Bad Habits

How to Train Your Mind and Body to Eliminate Bad Habits

(Unlock Your True Potential With Self Discipline Habits That Will Last Forever)

David Black

I0095508

Published By **Jordan Levy**

David Black

All Rights Reserved

Bad Habits: How to Train Your Mind and Body to Eliminate Bad Habits (Unlock Your True Potential With Self Discipline Habits That Will Last Forever)

ISBN   978-1-998927-70-8

Legal & Disclaimer

Upon using the information contained in this book, you agree to hold harmless the Author from and against any damages, costs, and expenses, including any legal fees potentially resulting from the application of any of the information provided by this guide. This disclaimer applies to any damages or injury caused by the use and application, whether directly or indirectly, of any advice or information presented, whether for breach of contract, tort, negligence, personal injury, criminal intent, or under any other cause of action.

You agree to accept all risks of using the information presented inside this book. You need to consult a professional medical practitioner in order to ensure you are both able and healthy enough to participate in this program.

Table Of Contents

Chapter 1: How Habits Work

Habits are funny matters to behold if we detachedly test them and determine them. The irony in behavior lies inside the reality that it contradicts the announcing, "To destroy may be very smooth, however to create takes time," due to the fact conduct are as an opportunity tough to save you when they have been without trouble created.

What are behavior? According to the Merriam-Webster dictionary, conduct are behavior styles obtained through the use of frequent repetition or physiologic publicity that show themselves in regularity or elevated facility of standard performance. The 2d definition in step with identical dictionary is even greater insightful as it defines a addiction as, "an obtained mode of conduct that has turn out to be nearly or simply involuntary.

In an attempt to throw greater mild on what the word, "addiction" way, allow's look at some different definition with a slightly one of a kind attitude. According to the American Journal of Psychology", a dependancy, from the viewpoint of psychology, is a greater or an entire lot a whole lot much less constant way of questioning, willing, or feeling acquired through previous repetition of a intellectual revel in... Behavioral styles we repeat are imprinted in our neural pathways."

The popularity of the above definition is "intellectual revel in" and guidelines on the highbrow or emotional nature of behavior. Although conduct typically start off with strictly physical interest, they turn out to be lodged in our way of doing subjects on a intellectual degree and are quite capable of becoming a massive a part of our lives.

Now that the definitions are thoroughly out of the manner, we will take a critical have a look at habits and try and understand exactly how they paintings. A beneficial piece of literature at the problem is from Charles Duhigg, who, thru a systematic have a look at of rats in a maze end up able to create the hypothesis of Habit Loops. Before we bypass into his explanation in spite of the reality that, allow's see what the American Journal of Psychology explains as Habit Formation, which manifestly is the time period that suggests how conduct come to be involuntary (computerized).

In their terms, "As behaviors are repeated in a steady context, there is an incremental growth in the link the various context and the motion. This will growth the automaticity of the conduct in that context." In an entire lot lots much less complex terms, the above assertion technique that behaviors are moves which is probably repeated frequently and possibly well timed, and so, they get registered inside the brain.

Let me fast country that a touch statistics of the way the thoughts works is important for some components of the subsequent discourse. This is a brief summary of what I look at currently: the thoughts sends messages via nerves (neurons) and there are roads via which the messages are despatched, the ones roads are known as neural pathways. After the ones messages are despatched frequently, with none aware call for of such neurons from the brain, commands that set off such actions are despatched to elements of the frame that generally perform that repeated movement. A dependancy has been long-set up, for this reason. Efficiency, lack of understanding, unintentionality, and uncontrollability are a few capabilities of dependancy.

So a ways, we've got have been given looked at what addiction manner and concluded that it's miles intellectual-based totally. We have additionally seen that conduct are crafted from constructing blocks, a number of which can be motion and behavior (conduct includes feelings and willing), regularity, registry, unconscious and lack of control. We have to now check out this remarkable explanation from Charles Duhigg in his book, The Power of Habits: Why We Do What We Do in Life and Business. Permit me to offer a hint excerpt from his ebook:

The technique of converting a complicated series of actions into an automatic ordinary is called "chunking", and human brains perform a similar manner. They variety in complexity, from setting toothpaste in your toothbrush earlier than placing it to your mouth, to getting dressed or making equipped breakfast, to very complex strategies in conjunction with backing one's car out of the driveway. All of these actions first of all required huge attempt to check, however in the end they have become so automatic as to be completed without aware interest. As quick as we select out out the proper cue, together with pulling out the car keys, our mind activates the stored addiction and we ought to our conscious minds popularity on some component else. In order to keep attempt, the brain will strive to show nearly any habitual right right into a addiction.

The ultimate statement is the very purpose why we have were given got such a lot of conduct we need we have to eliminate; it's also the cause why conduct are so easy to create. Yes, the mind will (always) strive to show any everyday proper right into a addiction as it attempts its best to be an green organ. Also, due to the fact we create sports activities for ourselves quite with out hassle, we therefore make it very clean for the brain to create behavior. In truth, every generation ensures that the whole lot we do turns into a ordinary. You placed on a tv with the aid of the usage of urgent a button. You stress a car thru urgent down on pedals. You begin a vehicle by means of turning a key. You do a lot of these items the identical way every unmarried time and so it will become a recurring. Now, allow's take a look at the Habit Loop which says that dependancy are tied spherical three machine-points; Cue, Routine, and Reward.

Let's see if we will make enjoy of this loop thru explaining what each time length manner and the way they deliver an motive of the phenomenon of dependancy formation. First, the Cue. Just similar to the literal which means that of the word, cue is the sign for whilst an motion ought to start. Before the mind begins offevolved sending a "registered" movement, it goals a signal. So the thoughts registers a cue and right away that cue is seen, the motion (dependancy) is introduced about into movement. The thoughts makes use of cues to keep away from the triggering of a dependancy continuously and so that after we want our conduct to be delivered on in motion, there may be no stalling and no attempt to research

The ordinary is the following part of the addiction loop and bodily sports are connected. This is what's added about via the thoughts on seeing the cue. The collection or collection of movements which is probably began out via the thoughts is referred to as the ordinary. In specific phrases, the routine is the addiction.

Reward, is the closing way point at the loop. It is that this aspect that ensures that the primary get registered within the first location. Remember, that human beings are burdened out for self-maintenance because of this that that instinctively, the thoughts will constantly appearance out to avoid risk. So, to avoid registering any regular that endangers the character, the thoughts analyses the result of sports. If the quit result of the thoughts's short check makes the character feels true, he may ask for it once more. If no longer, it's far taken for consideration at the registry. In specific phrases, if the end result is proper, the mind will keep it to be repeated. If no longer, the mind will discard it. In exceptional terms, all behavior, whether or not or now not or not they have got horrific results ultimately or not, leave the doer feeling suitable right away after it's miles finished.

Summarily then, that is how behavior work: Actions, mind, feelings take area as soon as. The mind takes be aware of what introduced at the motion and the stop end result. If the movement is repeated over and over, the brain registers it as a routine. Once the everyday is taken into consideration to be worthwhile, the brain, in a bid to store attempt, registers a neural pathway that lets in the individual carry out the motion sub-consciously, and every now and then, uncontrollably.

Chapter 2: How To Delete A Bad Habit

The first addiction we need to delete is the dependancy of wondering that dependancy is a awful word in its ordinary revel in. There are correct behavior and there are horrible behavior and there are impartial conduct. According to Mr. Duhigg, "conduct are crucial to our capacity to characteristic. People with damage to the basal ganglia, the elements of the mind liable for everyday behavior, regularly turn out to be mentally paralyzed."

It is likewise well worth of study that each one conduct are evaluated through the usage of our brains to make certain that no straight away risk is introduced upon our physical properly-being. Therefore, every suitable conduct and terrible habits supply a right away "feel-correct" sensation earlier than they get registered via our brains. Partly due to this, lousy conduct can also feel in reality "appropriate" and every so often may be reinterpreted because of how they make us feel.

However, horrific behavior might also moreover and do result in long term lousy outcomes, physical, socially, psychologically or maybe emotionally. Now that we've set up that horrible conduct are lousy in every revel in and excellent enjoy real, we are capable of move in advance to attention on a few awful behavior that plague us as human beings. Some of the maximum common lousy behavior available encompass: procrastination, laziness, lousy hygiene behavior, anger, lateness, late night time time snacking, consuming junk, smoking, binge ingesting and others. The without delay delight brought about with the beneficial useful resource of those behavior cover the deep-rooted problems which they carry of their wake.

Bad behavior are the ones which, in the long time, defeat our functions or goals. The essential factor isn't how they experience within the meantime however the effect they have on our lives in destiny. Sometimes, terrible conduct are the exceptional aspect standing in the manner of our turning into the correct humans we would really like to be. The query then is, how will we conquer them?

This question could be very vital because of the reality it's far one asked with the useful resource of using masses of human beings every day. The second humans understand they've terrible behavior and are able to realize how the ones terrible behavior have an effect on them detrimentally, their interest right away turns to getting rid of the ones awful habits.

Before answering the question thinking about how to conquer horrible conduct, I'd need to kingdom that out of understand for my readers, I do now not proclaim any brief fixes nor will I attempt to sugarcoat the facts; I will inform things like they are and do my very best to help you get out of the rut of lousy conduct in case you're already in it.

The first hassle we need to undergo in mind in in search of to conquer a horrible addiction is to apprehend that THEY CANNOT BE STOPPED EXACTLY. They may be exchanged but they can't be stopped. What does that mean? Once the thoughts has saved a addiction loop, it turns into quite hard with a view to forget about about the cue which triggers the habitual. Remember 3 capabilities of dependancy include, "lack of awareness, unintentionality and uncontrollability." It's like setting a spoon of ice cream for your tongue and seeking to forestall yourself from savoring the taste. It can be quite an exhausting mission to do that. So, in preference to seeking to prevent yourself from savoring the flavor – and failing woefully – you can as a substitute placed a spoon of vegetable soup on your tongue.

Seeing as lousy conduct can not be stopped, our attention shouldn't be on attempting to find to transport a wall however rather the way to get spherical it. To do this correctly, we've got to investigate the addiction loop of that particular dependancy after which focus specifically at the cue and the praise.

Let's use one unique terrible dependancy as our case have a have a look at to demonstrate this factor; a video game dependancy for example. Imagine a person who owns a video game console at home and plays it a lot, he has time for not anything else. Now, allow's create a routine. Once the online game addict comes domestic, the primary notion that crosses his thoughts is the video game. So, the subsequent movement the addict plays is a mad dash to the video game console to place it on. He performs the sport for hours, without being attentive to some thing else, whether or not meals or chores or university paintings until a person yells at him. It is best at this point, that he disconnects himself and receives up to transport away the sport on my own.

To emerge as aware about the cue which reasons the addict to at once obtain for the console the instantaneous he gets home, the surroundings is fundamental. It's obvious that the sport cannot have a hold over him out of doors the house. It's additionally obvious that it's miles most effective even as he's by myself and with out supervision that he can get entry to the online game. The ordinary is walking to the sitting room, pushing the energy button of each the console and television, and then choosing up the manipulate pad. The praise is the texture-proper sensation that comes from attractive in the online game interplay. Remember that it will now not be clean for the character with the addiction to analyze this loop due to the fact it's miles unconscious and he/she could be too busy taking component within the motions and sensations. It takes time and deliberateness to gain this evaluation. However, as quickly as this has been performed, the following step can be to change the habitual inside the addiction loop.

To obtain this, the first step might be to arrange or trade the environment. Remove the sport console from in which it have become. Preferably, mounted an area wherein it'll take some super time to get it out and join it. The conscious try of bringing out the game and connecting it'll smash the ordinary nature of the addiction. Within that thing, you can then determine which you in truth don't need to play the sport, at the least not inside the imply time at the identical time as you must be targeted on a few factor more critical, like a home art work. However, because of the reality loop awaits a praise, if that place for ordinary is left putting, the body will enjoy like a few component is missing. It turns into careworn until the loop is completed. So, there is a want to replace that recurring with some issue for you to be extra healthful but will go away a fantastic feeling. You may additionally located a crossword puzzle within the sitting room, in order that right away you run to the vicinity, while you do not see the sport console, you choose out up the puzzle or some special issue, and do for some time. Obviously, you acquired't play the puzzle for extended.

Another method of deleting a lousy addiction is removing the cue or the difficulty which triggers the ordinary. Using our above case check, in which the cue is electrical electricity approaching, you may determine to cast off the bulb or fan or some thing that cues you to the reality that power has now been restored. The extra we complicate the dependancy loop, the a great deal less the brain is able to be part of up it proper proper into a addiction.

Practically, we understand that it is probably more difficult than this to alternate lousy conduct but the extremely good news is that when we stay with the brand new recurring, it turns into the dependancy. So, like we stated at the onset of this situation rely, there are correct conduct as well as lousy conduct. To prevent a awful addiction, update it with a brilliant habit. The brain can not tell the difference, it only registers it within the neural pathway. And just like computers, garbage-in, rubbish-out. It all is primarily based upon on our enter.

However, we must be careful no longer to reengineer the vintage surroundings or cue, due to the fact mind stores every habit loop and does now not delete them, regardless of the fact that they're no longer used for a long term. So, as fast as an antique cue is engaged, the dependancy loop kicks off over again. Which is what is known as relapse. In looking to prevent habits, trade friends, exchange hangouts, alternate surroundings, alternate house arrangements because all this stuff may be cues for a terrible addiction.

Chapter 3: How To Create New Habits

To apprehend the way to create new conduct, allow's go decrease decrease again to the motive given through manner of the American Journal of Psychology on addiction formation, "as behaviors are repeated in a everyday context, there may be an incremental boom inside the link the various context and the movement. This will increase the automation of the conduct in that context." At the begin of this article, we simplified this explanation. We will benefit this all another time via saying; frequency begets automaticity. The greater frequent an movement, the more likely the mind will make it automated. The motive for this is that the thoughts reduces the attempt of recognition thru doing topics subconsciously.

Another reason why behavior motive us issues whilst we strive to interrupt them is that the praise we get from such everyday turns into a craving once the cue is triggered and the routine does no longer observe. The body becomes harassed as it has recognized that cue with an predicted result. How do I simplify this similarly? In every employer that each person would endure in mind going into, the praise is generally the pinnacle interest. That's exactly what the brain does in turning a ordinary proper proper right into a addiction. To create a new dependancy, we have to consider the praise the mind will sign up. For example, if we need to make waking up by the usage of five a dependancy, getting ready a warmth espresso and taking it with some cookies each time we awaken with the useful resource of five. Once the thoughts notices that there can be a reward for that everyday, the cue for waking up will become 5'o clock.

In the film, Three Idiot, the principle man or woman said, "The thoughts is simple to mislead." Once you are crucial approximately developing a brand new addiction, select a cue or cause, follow it up with routine (dependancy) you'll want to create after which reward your self with something that brings about a sense pinnacle sensation to the thoughts. It may be a few difficulty the least bit. From some thing as cheaper as verbal self-talk or blow his own trumpet, to an expensive meal in five-celeb inn. Once you may preserve doing a habitual, the mind will speedy take a look at in it inside the neural pathway and bam! You will speedy be doing it with out taking into account it.

It is however advocated that we don't pick out out any praise at the manner to quickly come to be lousy to us ultimately. For instance, choosing to praise your self with junk food for any time you run a kilometer, or taking a big chew out of our monetary savings to have a good time an fulfillment. Just don't forget that irrespective of how small the reward is the brain will check in it into the loop.

The genuinely smooth element about the neural pathway is that "even as a addiction becomes sufficiently installed in the mind, the cue not virtually turns on the ordinary - it additionally makes us crave the reward that is associated with completing the everyday. If the cue is gift, however we can't have interaction inside the routine or try to save you ourselves from doing so, the craving will increase in energy till it turns into almost overpowering."

This is why behavior come to be uncontrollable and sometimes, unintentional. This is each an great element and a awful detail. At the onset of making a brand new addiction, we typically complain about the try it takes to, for instance, wake up early, put together the children for college, put together ourselves for art work, skip through all that dreary internet site visitors and get to the place of business to fulfill a few worrying colleagues and boss. So, we popularity on the horrible emotions that we get from doing this, every weekday, and each day, we wake up with a unhappy head to head a dreary day. However, if we start to see the ones sports sports as sports, what we surely want to do is area numerous cues for each set of ordinary and a reward for every of them and soon, regardless of the truth that we burn up the identical amount of power doing it every day, it will become unconscious (regular) and we're capable of awareness on wonderful extra uplifting or thrilling activities on the equal time as our body perform the sports. Therein lies the difference amongst a satisfied administrative center person and a moody colleague. Strangely, the moody colleague will constantly marvel, "How does he do it?"

The difficulty is as soon as this dependancy (of making prepared and going to the office every weekday) has been normal, it stays a dependancy for each weekday, even supposing one is on go away, ill leave or excursion. That is why maximum retirees who absolutely loved their art work commonly find out it tough to simply live domestic and loosen up. Their body and mind keep longing for the sports and the worthwhile emotions which it's been privy to through the years. Most people grow to be going to look for every other hobby, even as what they need to have simply completed is replace the exercises within the addiction loop, leave the cues and the rewards in vicinity. For example, in choice to look for a hobby to update the vintage one, search for every different interest as a manner to although result in the same profitable sensation as the quality you get from finishing a business company interest in the administrative center.

Summarily, the decision of the sport of creating a modern day addiction is understanding how antique ones have been lengthy-hooked up. According to Duhigg, more human beings might have the ability to conquer their terrible behavior and create new, more healthy ones, if most effective they understood the addiction loop of that precise dependancy. Cues. Routine. Reward. It doesn't depend if the modern addiction is to update an antique one or to start afresh, definitely make it a routine that is delivered on with the useful useful resource of whatever that is repeatable and make sure to prevent it with a praise to yourself. The mind will take it up from there.

Chapter 4: How Habits Can Change Your Life

Just as described at the begin of this e-book, the thoughts tries as a whole lot as viable to lessen efforts with the aid of way of turning carrying sports to behavior. The implication of this is that most of what we do each day grow to be our behavior, in spite of the reality that we may not realise it. Bathing, brushing, consuming, praying, sitting, reputation, walking, using and loads of numerous mundane topics we do. However, there are one of a kind fundamental or minor behavior we expand alongside the manner, that we do no longer even consider, that makes us specific. These conduct have come to be our individual and it's far the ones conduct which have saved or brought us to in which we are. You need to have study various books that stated "conduct" of successful human beings. What does ebook won't deliver to your phrase is that a number of these conduct have been not got all the way down to be finished with the useful resource of those a achievement human beings, consciously. Neither had been they born with them. They can also were educated that manner, or they may have decided to act that way again and again and the mind stored it to grow to be a addiction.

Habits like timeliness, integrity, dishonesty, cleanliness, decency, verbal morality, dressing, nail-biting, gum-chewing, shouting, screaming, speakme softly, and so forth, all have one difficulty in common. They are achieved without conscious try and while we may additionally moreover deliver excuses that essentially argue that it's virtually "who I am" or inform pals that they need to "take me the way I am or leave" or declare that "I can't change who I am," the truth is that you simply can trade. The easy reason is that you have been as quickly as without the ones behavior. We didn't pop out from our mother's womb, telling lies or screaming down everyone to get to paintings and give you consequences! Rather than are seeking out to stop a dependancy, attempting to find to turn out to be what you've got been in advance than the addiction. The problem proper here, but, is how do conduct exchange our lives?

Successful people had been possibly now not continuously a fulfillment, as a minimum that's what maximum in their biographies inform us. Some turned into once failures or smooth mediocre. The identical goes for unsuccessful or everyday human beings. Most want to have completed excellently at the same time as in faculty or university, however all of a stunning they become mediocre. What took place earlier than the alternate in reputation (a fulfillment/ordinary) changed right right into a exchange of addiction. Those humans began out doing what they were now not doing in advance than. Someone as soon as said, "You can't be doing precisely what you've been doing and assume a notable cease quit result," at least not inside the long term. People who triumph over unwanted situations along aspect weight loss, health education, anger control, dependancy rehabilitation have all succeeded for one clean purpose. They modified their conduct.

So how did addiction change their lives? First, behavior, even though can be mentally blamed on the thoughts (for registering it and eliminating our manipulate), it is we who first started out the motion and persevered it earlier than the thoughts helped us out. The first step is self-evaluation. What do you do not forget yourself? Does your actual character come close to your satisfactory individual? We all have a mental photograph of what we would want to end up. But lifestyles takes place and we don't come to be exactly that picture, however a success humans come a whole lot in the direction of that photograph via way of looking to do the proper difficulty. It starts offevolved with their approach. It changed into Socrates that stated, "I expect, therefore I am." What we consider ourselves determines what we do. If assume I am an honest character, as plenty as possible (probable now not all the time), I inform it the way it is. If I see myself as an impeccable cloth cabinet, I try no longer to compromise in that regards. Our concept strategies moreover turns into a dependancy. Honest people effects, maximum instances, inform it the manner it is. So, if we ought to do the right issue, we want to suppose the right component.

The 2d step to having behavior alternate our lives is doing what we preserve forth (to ourselves, at the least). This may not be hundred percentage, however we need to in no manner allow the few times we fail ourselves spoil all the instances we have been a success. When we are announcing we don't insult human beings and something makes us do it. We want to now not let that slip stop us from trying or making efforts to turning into the proper us. Live for each day. And consider to reward yourself whenever you achieve success at it. This manner the mind takes the effort a long way from us. Remember when you commenced to stress. You notion times approximately it earlier than transferring that gadget or taking your foot some distance from the seize. Today, but, you do all of these motion and force at 70kmp while considering what to inform your boss so that you can take the following break day. One may additionally ask, what changed into the praise we gave ourselves whilst we were mastering to pressure? The answer is the delight of wearing out what you concept you in no way ought to, modified into one. Another question is, what praise does the mind however get from the use of now that you don't undergo in mind it or see it as a large deal? You never can tell now, for wonderful, because of the fact it's far now subconscious however you may ensure that the thoughts remains getting its reward. The thoughts has created a pathway. That's the equal way your life modifications at the same time as you begin to create new behavior. At first, it's far very hard. You pressure yourself to say the truth. You pressure yourself to save you selecting your nose; you are taking a deep breath and just drum your "choosy finger" to your palm. And then, your mind receives that, "Yes, I didn't choose it!" That silent scream makes you want to upward push above it over and over once more. Soon, you don't even recognise that your life has changed.

Just as clean as it's miles to change our lives for suitable through changing our conduct, we also can trade our lives for worse via those equal techniques of dependancy formation. It is therefore important to perform self-examination frequently to appearance in case you are absolutely drawing toward becoming the proper you. Don't be glad with the straight away give up result of now not entering into hassle or for reducing corners to acquire the prevent, it actually is falsely assumed to justify the manner. You may additionally have a better existence than you do, now. Change what you do, grade by grade and soon, you will become the modern-day and higher you.

Chapter 5: How Long Does It Take To Create Habits?

In seeking to recognize how lengthy it takes to shape a addiction, you need to think about the individuality of individuals. You need to in no way diploma a while with the subsequent individual who is moreover looking to shape the identical dependancy as you. Some things you have to undergo in mind are; first, the brains of different people paintings in another manner. For example, some humans are extra photographic and could do not forget to do matters greater without difficulty than the following character. Secondly, consistency differs among humans. Some human beings can be diligent in their zeal to shape a addiction and so, it may take them, allow's say, forty days, on the same time as others who are not regular will although form that identical addiction after eighty days. That stated, scientifically, it takes a median of

66 days (2 months) to shape a dependancy. Remember, the key-word is common. This technique it is able to take greater or lots much much less than the quantity of days indexed above.

The unique information is that missing an afternoon or at the same time as looking for to shape a dependancy does now not propose you want to start at some stage in. Thank heavens the mind is more clever than that, in any other case some of us may want to in no way shape any addiction. There become a idea that it took 21 days to form a dependancy. This end up everyday as a truth through human beings whilst a standard practitioner, Maxwell Maltz, postulated it through looking at his patients and himself. However, these days, that hypothesis has been dispelled with the aid of way of using a research completed with the aid of a institution of scientists at the University College London.

Habit formation isn't always a one-off thingy where you clearly anticipate the thoughts to create a pattern and join up it right now you begin. Otherwise, the entirety we do will become a dependancy. And this long time it takes to form a addiction is what leaves room for relapse for the ones searching for to update a awful dependancy with a modern-day one. However, I receive as real with that one detail in an effort to make the mind shape a addiction more rapid is reward. Just the same manner, a little one is more likely to replicate a super act or behavior due to the fact he continues to get rewards for whenever he does, the mind is much more likely to sign on a habitual that effects in smooth outcomes. A story is counseled of strategies Pepsodent made brushing a dependancy for optimum people through manner of inclusive of citric acid to toothpaste which left a tingly feeling at the enamel and gum after brushing; that is a conventional instance.

This is what maximum groups do in recent times; they make certain that the customer is left with a direct worthwhile sensation for the use of their products or services and this makes them get hooked on it. Companies in America like MacDonald's and different consumable items producers work with this concept. The query as to how quick human beings end up everyday customers is debatable or speculative but one hassle is wonderful. A client is much more likely to patronize over again, that appropriate that leaves him proper away feeling well than that which takes an extended time to expose up its impact.

Bearing this in mind, we must mission to praise carrying events which we preference to transform into behavior. Most humans find out it hard to formulate the dependancy because of the fact they offer an extended place of time among physical games and rewards and but they assume it to stick quicker. Some waste treasured time beating up themselves for slip-usainstead of worthwhile themselves for the little milestones they add to their efforts every distinctive day. I can can help you recognize from private revel in that the carrot method beats the stick technique any time, any day.

I expect as soon as the praise machine is actually addressed, it's going to take a shorter time to formulate that addiction. Likewise, as quickly as the reward tool is omitted and inadequately addressed, then one must in all likelihood anticipate an prolonged length to formulate that addiction. From the identical research completed above, it's miles stated that it

41

took a few individuals as a superb deal as 254 days to shape a habit. I trust it's miles due to the fact the people in query were greater focused at the habitual and in no manner even considered cues and rewards. The thriller in the again of creating or breaking habits lie, at the whole, in records the addiction loop. The quicker you're able to analyze successfully a selected addiction loop, the faster you're able to break this type of dependancy. The equal is going for making a modern-day dependancy each to replace the antique one or start a present day one afresh.

Another difficulty to take into account in developing conduct is the complexity of the addiction in query. The more complicated the ordinary, the longer you may must be at it for the mind to check in it. This is due to the fact even you, who consciously plays this interest, also can overlook part of the recurring alongside the street, until it is written. And if you have to take a look at it to don't forget it, it need to turn out to be even more hard to memorize it. So the answer may be to break a complex ordinary into smaller ones, with cues coming inside and the praise coming at the very stop. However, you may create verbal rewards for each new cue and recurring together with verbal self-talk or sing his own praises. The important issue stays that you make it less tough for the mind to conceptualize. For instance, if you want to shape the addiction of bathing without delay you return backtrack out of your bed, you may located your tub slips and towel very close to your bed, so the primary component you put on, on stepping down out of your bed is your bath slip and towel. The praise for bathing need to now not proper away be a cup of espresso if you want your routine to be complicated to the element of stepping into the bus earlier than a selected time. Rather, the profitable cup of espresso should come while you're ultimately seated at the bus.

Chapter 6: How And When To Introduce Your Next Habit

Old conduct stick around actual lengthy or maybe while we attempt to put off them, it's hard to forestall them with out options. Does this advocate that if we intend to prevent an vintage, awful addiction, then our excellent bet is to opportunity it with every other lousy dependancy?

Not actually, so do no longer be alarmed. I'm definitely seeking to factor out that each addiction, whether or no longer horrible or nicely fulfills a need and the motive our our bodies crave for horrific behavior we're looking to discard and usually run again to them is because of the want the terrible behavior were first-class.

This can appear daunting but it is able to be done. The reputation in phrases of dropping a awful dependancy shouldn't be in truth discarding it but converting it with a healthful addiction which fulfills the equal want. This method a cutting-edge dependancy need to be brought even as you're running on giving up an vintage one.

To illustrate, permit me provide an example. After an extended day at work, someone comes home and badly in want of some thing to relax him, takes more than one pics of scotch. They lighten up him, of path, but he finally ends up with the dependancy of eating scotch approximately 6 days every week and he is aware of that it's a horrible hassle. Trying to remove the ingesting might be difficult – specially considering he although goes to work and is derived once more confused out – so what is the manner out for him?

The solution is to strive losing the eating dependancy at the identical time as substituting it with a few issue so one can further lighten up him. He must attempt taking an extended, soaking tub whilst gets home or he need to engage in a bit walk out of doors his residence.

Regardless of what new approach he alternatives, he'll find out that it's a lot much less complicated to ditch ingesting as speedy as he has a few component that does what ingesting used to do for him. This explains why nicotine patches and e-cigarettes are recommended for individuals who are trying to find to stop smoking.

The following are hints detailing how you may introduce your new dependancy successfully:

-        Use timelines well: A timeline is a length you region for yourself as a hard manual or estimate to letting flow of your vintage dependancy. During this time, you can inject new workouts into your behavior. Since there can be no desired time body for every person coping with a dependancy – and their bodies – to efficiently kick out a terrible addiction, you need to pace yourself and not attempt to skip too speedy. Analyzing your one-of-a-kind, gift conduct can also offer you with notion into what governs your conduct and why you picked them up. Whether suitable or horrible, there was a reason, and now that you want to drop it, you need to have a purpose. Go ahead and inform your self that it will probably be top notch in the end. Timelines are critical due to the truth they arrive up with an predicted time of success and because of the reality they'll be quite sensible. Trying to forestall an antique addiction with out setting a time restrict can seem overwhelming to you so provide your self a proposed cease date after which begin. It can be 10 days or 2 weeks or every different low-fee matters to engage in. You don't even should attempt a addiction with the useful resource of way of going all of the way; you may start with a bit motive – through stopping a part of the dependancy and then persevering with from there.

- Don't Be Scared to Start Small: When introducing a new dependancy, now and again massive steps paintings in competition to us. We need to be inclined and affected man or woman enough to recognise that very tiny steps are rather powerful if we'd deliver them the time of day. Introducing a trendy addiction in tiny bits works very well and every body seeking to start one should internalize this factor. For example, if you intend to devour plenty tons much less and additional wholesome, you don't should wake up one Monday morning and attempt an intensive exchange to your eating addiction. You must start by means of way of notwithstanding the truth that eating your dangerous meals however in little quantities. When you've gotten used to eating smaller portions, you may then begin to add in healthful food additives like greens, fish and fruit.

-      Introduce new behavior one after the other: If you find out your self inside the middle of multiple horrible behavior and feel a pressing need to drop them, the high-quality way can be to drop them one after the alternative and then introducing new behavior one after the opposite. The brain can also moreover theoretically have an almost endless quantity of storage (which we've been not capable of faucet) however close to frequent sports like conduct, the segment in rate is quite finite. Our conduct are our commonplace sports activities and the segment of the thoughts in rate of our behavior is the prefrontal cortex. The prefrontal cortex is much like the RAM in a computer in particular in a single place – its memory is finite. The prefrontal cortex can efficiently cope with best a number of requirements in advance than it starts offevolved offevolved to stumble upon problems. These problems appear within the body in the shape of feelings like fatigue or maybe anger. This is defined thru the prefrontal cortex's sturdy hyperlink with the amygdala. The amygdala is the emotional middle of the brain – some pupils talk over with it as primitive – and it's miles the a part of the mind which controls our body's fight or flight response. It's been suggested that the prefrontal cortex gets without problem worn-out and overloaded and therefore, we do not apprehend benevolent recommendation as such and as an alternative react to it through getting at the protective.

Considering that it's far this equal prefrontal cortex that handles conduct, it's clean why losing a couple of ones or studying more than one ones right away is a large task for anyone. Therefore if you set a intention for yourself that goes a few difficulty like, "From subsequent week, I'll start using the steps, prevent smoking cigarettes and stop poking my nose in public", you'll maximum in all likelihood fail to advantage it. The exceptional way to gain all the above is to address them in my opinion, one after the opposite.

If you study those steps, you'll fast be to your way to discarding those behavior you don't like and converting them with new, healthy conduct.

Chapter 7: How To Make A Habit Permanent

It is an established truth that developing or breaking a addiction isn't always precisely an clean issue to do. While it has been said by means of the usage of way of numerous sources that a dependancy can be picked up with consistent exercise after a length of approximately 3 weeks, new information shows that it would actually take longer than that.

It has been recommended that for behavior to without a doubt grow to be a part of a person's life, to the factor in which the actions come to be truely computerized, they ought to be finished generally for a duration of about 2 months.

For the ones who've attempted to break a dependancy or replace it with a ultra-modern one, you understand how difficult it's miles to make a dependancy, in particular while you're creating a aware try. Many human beings might probable get to the factor of mastering those movements however first-rate few truely hit the quantity wherein they begin to perform them unconsciously.

Considering how a bargain of a assignment it's miles to either make a addiction or break it, how do you ensure that the brand new, healthy behavior you need to choose up stay with you genuinely? The following steps will help in getting you to the point in which your moves become a part of your unconscious and thereby, eternal:

-        Get yourself enormously recommended: If you're looking for to make a dependancy for your self and intend to hold it going in reality, you want to have motivation this is robust sufficient to get you there. Every change comes because of motivation and that is relevant to behavior too. To have an concept how nicely your quest for a brand new addiction will go, quietly test your primary motivation for wanting to select up this dependancy. If it isn't a effective, intrinsic one, then it's probably your quest will fall brief of your expectation. Extrinsic motivators are not that awful however they have got a first-rate disadvantage: they burnout real short. To problematic, I'll offer an instance. If you started out running out and lifting weights to look ripped so that you can provoke an extended-time overwhelm on an drawing near date, you'll in all likelihood education session nicely for some time. Then following your crush's recognition of you and a recognition that her appeal for you has nothing to do in conjunction with your looks or body type, your motivation is likely to drop. Going to the gym will not be quite a few a topic for you and as such, you would possibly prevent running out surely and bypass all over again to the shape you had been in earlier than. If on the other hand, you started out out walking out because you believed it was part of wholesome living and due to the fact you couldn't have enough cash – emotionally or otherwise – to be a victim of coronary coronary heart disorder, you'd likely workout to the most. Even if you neglected multiple days, remembering the reason you began out receives you lower back rapid enough.

-        Make a nicely laid-out plan: It is probably cliché at this issue but a amazing quote that applies to almost every concern count number out there is going as a quit result, "If you fail to prepare, you are making organized to fail." When it involves making your addiction stay completely, you need a calculated route of motion and also you need to stay with the plan to help you accumulate your reason. A plan permits   for remarkable if you have executed what you meant and additionally specifies what boundaries you want to no longer exceed. This all sounds easy to maintain track off however in reality, matters art work higher at the same time as we positioned them to paper and no longer really leave them in our heads. So it's without a doubt useful, vital even, which you write down your plan for developing your new addiction, irrespective of how tedious or silly it would seem. The plan you create desires to be very seen so stick it in your fridge or vicinity it inside the groove of your bed room mirror, door of your material cloth wardrobe or everywhere you may be forced to see it. The plan additionally wishes to be particular, detailing what you'll do to efficaciously create the dependancy. This manner that famous, indistinct statements like "I will save you attending to artwork late" or "I will take a stroll" everyday will now not work and may best preserve you decrease decrease returned.

-        Be equipped to comply: If you're horrible at adapting, then at the equal time as looking for to create a dependancy, you'll need to inspire yourself to turn out to be very adaptable. Sometimes, inside the course of seeking to forge a present day addiction, we recognize that the technique we took wasn't the quality or that some part of the plan we wrote down wishes to be tweaked. When this takes location, it isn't a signal that the addiction we need is unrealistic or unachievable, it's in fact a name to movement to edit our plan and from there we are able to circulate on.

-        Take word of your triggers: In looking for to make a today's addiction eternal, we need to definitely first assault and damage an antique one. Breaking an vintage dependancy is often a vital step on the manner to forming a cutting-edge addiction and we want to be aware of some telltale signs and symptoms worried with our horrible conduct. Every horrible dependancy, properly ones too, typically have triggers that motive the character involved to crave for them or, if it's superior enough, begin to unconsciously perform the dependancy. These triggers are as numerous as there are humans in the global and for instance functions, a number of them are: the searching of sports sports video video games causing someone to drink beer, a terrible day at paintings inflicting a person to stroll into the pastry maintain and binge on cake, and an trouble with a spouse causing someone to stroll proper right into a online on line casino to gamble. The extra those triggers occur, the more the individual plays their horrific conduct. Studying and identifying triggers are very useful due to the truth right away the reason event occurs, the character is aware that the following thing to arise might be a push in the direction of the addiction and so they may be more organized to stand up to or divert their interest. Triggers paintings with incredible habits too and can be intentionally laid round to encourage. For instance, someone who has resolved to consume greater fruit, can lay the dining desk with fruit the night time time in advance than, absolutely so at ate breakfast, they're added approximately to devour fruit.

With regular exercise, strength of will and the exercise of those guidelines with out a exceptions, every body can make their new conduct come to be eternal.

Chapter 8: How To Stop Repeating The Same Mistakes

While we strive to certainly understand how we form conduct and the way they have an impact on our lives, it's pertinent to check mistakes and see how they emerge as part of our bad behavior.

We generally apprehend a mistake at the same time as we make one; we'd enjoy lousy or maybe angry approximately it after which we commonly promise ourselves we gained't reason them to another time. Few days or hours later, we discover ourselves repeating those errors. This can occur a couple of instances and just like that, a lousy addiction has been born.

We've probably all heard this pronouncing, "Doing the same trouble time and again even as looking for notable outcomes is an appropriate definition of insanity." So why do lots people preserve repeating our errors? I mean, we recognize they're errors or at the least matters that we'd need to forestall doing. We understand that they're now not wholesome for us and need not anything more than to examine our schooling and stroll far from those errors for proper. Why will we enjoy our mistakes hard? Or is it secure to count on that masses folks are downright insane but truely don't absolutely apprehend it?

What if there's a diffused cause that traps us on this repetitive sample and continues us from breaking free? We is probably privy to the life of this problem however are we aware about the idea reason?

By an intention reputation of the reasons behind our errors, we are capable of lock at once to the motive of our cyclical mistake styles and prevent them. The following steps can guide us:

-       Fully turn out to be aware about the error you hold repeating: In our anger and melancholy at our tendency to continuously repeat our errors, we on occasion overlook approximately approximately the severity or totality of the mistakes we devote. This is flawlessly normal and with a touch education and statement, we can select up at the mistakes we make all of the time. I once had an enjoy in an office surroundings, I became eager on referring files in a incorrect order and this commonly extended the time for assessment of the report. I modified into meant to talk over with Mr. C who would probable then send it along to Mr. G. I made a dependancy of referring it to Mr. G first; he need to have long beyond nearly midway through the document in advance than knowledge Mr. C hadn't seen it. It could likely have to be lower again and I emerge as called out severally for it. I didn't similar to the reality that I didn't appear to be learning but there regarded to be not some thing I should do approximately it. Months later, I decided out I had made a mistake inside the coding machine for his or her names and so couldn't generally inform who become who.

- Identify the reason at the back of your repetitive mistake: Rarely do people do subjects randomly and that is applicable to even actions they didn't intend to do, in any other case known as errors. If there are motives for the errors you commit, then it follows that till you're certainly aware about those reasons, you could hold aimlessly and unknowingly committing the ones errors. These reasons can quality be placed with the aid of manner of way of those within the state of affairs; we have to try to discover them out ourselves and no longer depart them to a few outdoor expert. If you mistakenly leave your key to your car because of the truth you're typically dashing to keep away from overdue, then until you prevent showing up overdue, you're at risk of all the time dashing and leaving your key within the ignition. Once you're able to restore your mistake of waking up late, you'll be in a better feature to be calm even as leaving your automobile and therefore will forestall leaving your key in it.

-        Start replacing as rapid as feasible: The 2d you discover a mistake, your immediately reaction need to be to replace it. Replacing it need to be the safety mechanism we hire however commonly, we don't realize any higher. (This should be your approach due to the fact it's far the simplest one which works). If you permit the error be, it'll virtually fester and turn into a big trouble which you may not be resultseasily able to address inside the destiny. Obsessing over the errors isn't a terrific idea either. Obsessing over the error you made and beating your self about it is probably your herbal reaction to the mistake but it excellent allows to reinforce the error, thereby unconsciously making you repeat them in the long run.

-     Make and preserve the adjustments: Finally, to stop making the ones mistakes, you have to impact the adjustments with the intention to maintain the errors out. If you maintain tune of whilst those errors generally get up, you may protect your self and seize yourself earlier than you slip into the sample. Thinking ahead is likewise a great manner to hold the modifications you're making; in case you are capable of appearance in advance and count on conditions in that you can repeat your errors, you'll be better geared up to save you yourself from making them. Stay satisfactory all of the time and comprehend that in case you slip-up as soon as, it doesn't imply you've failed. This is one in all the maximum essential obstacles humans come upon, in fact. While forging in advance, inside the event that they by chance fall off for a second, they pass lower lower back to bashing themselves, keep in thoughts themselves unworthy and prevent trying altogether.

Nobody's ideal; it's part of what makes us human. Our lack of perfection approach we'll make mistakes and it's never a lousy component until we repeat them over and over all another time and make no try and get away the vicious cycle. If you're ready to put in a bit art work, you may prevent your self from making the identical errors again and again another time.

Chapter 9: The Action Plan

Is exchange an splendid detail or a horrible issue? If you spoke back, "It depends on the state of affairs", you're very accurate. Beyond the "rightness" or "wrongness" of it despite the fact that, trade takes place constantly. It doesn't depend range what you think about alternate; you really need to accept that it's far an ever-present part of our fact.

We all should deal with change often and our attitude in the route of it determines, to a degree, the quality of our lives. Our regular touch with trade is pondered truely in our behavior. We unconsciously choose up new ones and adjust vintage ones all of the time. What we need to aspire to do, is to be more on pinnacle of things, and in order to alternate our terrible behavior as fast as we discover them, all on a conscious level.

Many parents attempt their utmost amazing to change their lousy conduct multiple instances however there aren't as many fulfillment memories as there have to be. It seems to be a as an opportunity daunting project and even folks who start the adventure seem to not often make it to the very prevent.

I understand a person who didn't take into account in any alternate of any kind. It become always humorous to him that human beings have to try to change their conduct. He could likely constantly say, "Our conduct are a part of us, whether or not or no longer awful or perfect. We're stuck with them and trying to trade them is like looking to change our very skin. Good proper fortune with that!"

I became very greater younger as soon as I knew this man and every time he raised this factor, I'd ponder it deeply to peer if he can be proper. I wasn't positive but I in no way countered him because of the fact I didn't want to reap a tongue-lashing. The guy moved faraway from our network in the end however from time to time I'd bear in mind his terms.

Years later, after encountering a few realistic men, masses of studies and a couple of mentoring lessons, I knew one-of-a-type. I have become glad that now not first-rate have been behavior located out however they'll be changed or modified. Unfortunately, I in no way met the "no-trade" man all over again. I need I had even though; it would were my pleasure to break the incredible statistics to him.

I don't sincerely blame my old neighbor for being so skeptical approximately the possibility of conduct to be modified. He had visible many humans try and fail and some of them had been pretty famous; their unlucky reports as they tried to alternate their conduct had been stated to lots folks who lived spherical that place.

There became the skillful network barber, a pleasing elderly man who constantly smiled. He had inclined lungs butt even after he decided out, he even though smoked some sticks of cigarettes an afternoon. There come to be also the neighborhood grocery man; he have been recognized with coronary heart disorder a few years lower back however nevertheless deep fried his bird. In fact, he enjoyed hosting community cookouts, so he need to "spread the joy of fried bird."

I had in my view heard those men confess – generally beneath the conceal of a hearty snigger – that they in truth desired to save you their terrible conduct however ought to by no means conquer the urges and cravings they felt. Little surprise my vintage neighbor believed no longer some thing could be finished approximately conduct.

I'm glad that our lives are full of many, tiny choices, related to our behavior. The folks that stay existence in complete gadget with many successes and who rapid rebound when they fall are honestly parents which might be in massive detail on pinnacle of things in their options and behavior. If you may exercising manipulate over your conduct, you'll be capable of higher direct the picks you are making and be a higher person commonly.

If you sense you've struggled sufficient or if you're not interested in struggling all the way to the pinnacle, you can contain the subsequent movement plan into your existence and make certain being dominated via terrible conduct is left within the beyond, for specific.

-      Recognize the compulsive belongings you do: Literally, a factor it really is compulsive is a few element this is born out of a large urge or craving, and which normally is going in opposition to as a minimum one's conscious wishes. In psychology, compulsive conduct is one this is executed constantly or repetitively and which does not usually result in an real reward or pride. Regardless of the manner you view it, compulsive behavior is awful stuff. It's smooth to rationalize them and make excuses for such conduct but with deep, impartial mirrored image, you may spot compulsive conduct. You'll find out that they in no way make contributions clearly to you however take away large quantities of a while and do damage to your health. Also apprehend that even the maximum mundane stuff you do may be compulsive conduct. For example, it's miles very feasible to browse the net compulsively.

-        Isolate your awful conduct: Bad conduct have to be quarantined; there's no reason they need to be stored in entire view to infect your suitable thoughts. The sad factor about terrible conduct is, it's pretty tough to look them in yourself. Even at the same time as you do, it's easy to get on the protective or justify the terrible deeds whilst in fact, they're easy crap and nothing more. It's a awesome ball exercise in spite of the fact that, whilst splendid humans very personal these horrible conduct. According to Alain de Botton, "The satisfactory remedy for one's awful dispositions is to see them in motion in a few different person." Botton absolutely manner that the same lousy conduct that we'd criticize and component fingers at are usually invisible to us if they'll be located on us. Unfortunately, his announcement that they will be cured via seeing them on a person else is a hint exaggerated because of the fact as we've visible, curing or breaking lousy behavior isn't a very clean hobby. As a good deal as possible, we need to isolate awful conduct and the events that lead as much as them. If an trouble or altercation befell along with your companion and it leads you to get inebriated, you have to recognize it and isolate it. Remind your self that some subjects are beyond your manipulate and due to the fact they get up isn't always any reason that permits you to engage in compulsive conduct.

-      Replace your behavior; it's a whole lot much less complex that manner: It might be real that breaking a addiction is tough work however there is a manner. Replacing your habits is that way, and it's quite very easy, in assessment to trying to surrender a awful addiction. You might have been suggested to subject yourself and focus on giving up your horrible addiction however it isn't that easy.

Working on pleasant giving up that dependancy makes use of an entire of strength which is essentially wasted because dependancy formation just doesn't work that manner. Did it rise up to you that the dependancy you're looking for to eliminate would possibly have without a doubt modified a smooth habit? Well, that's the manner it actually works and getting into opposition to it's time-ingesting and not very powerful.

Other additives of the motion plan which is probably pretty self-explanatory in nature are indexed underneath:

-      Find effective motivations.

-      Strengthen your energy of mind.

-      Spend greater time with folks that apprehend how treasured it's far to squash horrible behavior.

- Set goals for yourself and write them proper down to preserve yourself constantly inspired.

- Approach your plan for converting your terrible conduct in a realistic way.

- Don't attempt to take big steps right now; settle for infant steps and rest confident that they clearly artwork.

- Do now not be ashamed or afraid to invite for help from friends, circle of relatives, co-people and experts.

- Reward yourself with a deal with that is unrelated to the awful addiction to avoid setting off the horrible chain of activities.

- Love your self unconditionally and be more forgiving whilst you're making errors or briefly burst off-music.

Chapter 10: What Are Habits?

I am fine simply on the perception of the phrase dependancy you're sure you recognise what it approach, however an essential query is whether or now not you understand the impact and form of have an impact on conduct have in all regions of our lives. When defining a dependancy, we remember it as a conduct or motion that someone repeats often and that they usually do subconsciously. When we are saying one has a positive dependancy it method we are speakme approximately their fixed way of wondering, feeling, or performing. One essential issue to install thoughts is that maximum behavior are never found through the individual that is displaying them because as mentioned they normally do them unconsciously or as an alternative in no manner interact in self-assessment while doing them.

The reality is that antique behavior are difficult to break and new behavior are difficult to form however the second you fulfill these duties then your existence absolutely modifications. What many won't recognise is that someone's existence in recent times is largely a sum of all their conduct and that how in form or out of it you are, it's far a result of your conduct. To positioned the whole thing for your lifestyles in region you can need to begin via maintaining behavior which is probably aligned to that desire.

My element of emphasis is at the idea that what you over and over do shapes the individual you are, what you're taking delivery of as real with in, and moreover your individual. We may also or may not be satisfied about the ones components of our lives presently however it's miles all inner our electricity to make a distinction. It is all about converting your habits and there are such masses of techniques to transport about that. By doing this you could without problem enhance their health, relationships, profession, and many others.

Habit formation might not be as clean as many consider but once you placed your all into it then you definitely in truth take off some of that hassle. Breaking a awful addiction has its non-public demanding situations simply as forming new behavior does. When you determined of breaking an vintage dependancy, we're looking at this unique habitual you've got were given been following for as prolonged because it has lasted and that you allowed it to be engrained deep internal and is form of part of you. Forming a latest dependancy however is all about introducing a few factor sincerely new into your lifestyles, you will war to locate a part of you that fully relates with it as a manner of making it sink.

If you want to understand how important conduct are in our lives then it permits to recollect them as the maximum influential factors of our actions and full life. All your actions, alternatives, and your way of life, commonly are surprisingly dictated with the useful resource of the usage of your conduct. They factor us in a direction and if you need to make sure of the satisfactory vacation spot then you honestly need to focus at the first-rate conduct.

Since behaviors, or a difficult and fast of behaviors, are matters which is probably usually done automatically without someone thinking about it, or consciously intending to do them, it gives you a difficult concept of the manner powerful they're. If you don't workout manipulate over them, then they will be likely to offer you a journey to anywhere in the worldwide through any reviews or conditions. With all desires and goals in mind you can honestly omit out at the proper bus without a doubt virtually due to the fact you couldn't preserve the shape of conduct essential for that adventure.

One issue to look at is your habits are not fantastic restricted to your behaviors however your thoughts also can grow to be your behavior. You can increase a dependancy whether or now not right or lousy without reputation and frequently for the terrible ones you handiest recognize them as soon because the harm has been executed. This indicates you methods essential it's far to constantly stay within the present and consider and in touch with each feeling, concept and motion that takes place on your lifestyles. You may not must be so judgmental about them however certainly be smart enough to determine what is proper and what isn't always for you.

Habits are important as they assist everyone of their each day lives due to the truth it can be quite tiresome to need to expect consciously and direct your intentions on the equal time as doing some thing. Think of conditions like taking breakfast, going to mattress at a selected time, taking a shower, following a specific course at the same time as using, the ones are ordinary practices that if we would ought to reflect onconsideration on each time we do them they become very stupid and tiresome. At this factor you want to be aware of the lifestyles of each exquisite and lousy behavior, wherein as masses as the coolest conduct simplify and gain your life, the lousy ones can be pretty negative.

To shape new conduct an character desires to generally positioned them in thoughts and moreover try to actively put into impact them. Have some type of reminders on your environment so one can make you don't forget your specific dependancy formation purpose. Filling your lifestyles with best the best behavior has been proved to be a secret to meaking our lives better in almost all elements. When you think of the most a fulfillment human beings like entrepreneurs, they've got made it to where they're nowadays through way of preserving positive forms of behavior. These acted as their important manual and supply of direction permitting them to make the right selections and options. It is therefore upon you to pick out types of behavior that form you into perfection. With addiction formation and breaking there is no short restore method and one has to exercise loads staying strength.

Chapter 11: Embracing Change

In addiction formation or breaking, one not unusual thing we're all probably to stumble upon, is change. To dispose of horrible conduct you have to go through a changing approach and this additionally applies in dependancy formation. Some human beings locate it very hard to encompass alternate, and this is the cause why we in no way make a whole lot improvement. Embracing exchange is a key step in dependancy formation and I anticipate it's miles very crucial to first studies what alternate is and the manner you could first-rate encompass it.

A person's functionality to deal with and flow with exchange is all of their mind and this basically approach your mind. What you keep in mind a particular change determines how amazing you are able to cope with it. The second you have got were given the strength to be on pinnacle of factors of all your mind then it turns into tons less tough that allows you to discover ways to embody change. It is stated that to have extra power for your lifestyles, then it's miles vital that you have a way of controlling your mind.

In some of conditions, no person ever feels real whilst they are counseled to exchange their way of doing things, either in their professional or non-public lifestyles. This is constantly so because it is our vintage approaches that experience as part of us and we revel in that breaking from vintage conduct and manner of thinking shatters our complete being. This isn't constantly so due to the fact trade is commonly part of us and it's far excellent thru embracing it that we open ourselves as a lot as better things in existence.

In all levels and ranges of lifestyles, the only people who live to tell the story are the ones who've the coronary heart to consist of change. They recognize it is through this that one will boom their charge via using manner of such as greater knowledge and talents. Everything inside the worldwide is constantly evolving or changing in a few manner and that is greater reason for us to learn how to well known exchange. There are instances while people are required to change their behaviors and conduct for them to in shape into situations and environments.

As someone you need to observe that change may be quite uncomfortable or very awkward, however by the usage of gaining knowledge of a way to effectively adapt to it, high-quality alternate will clearly have an impact to your life. There is a completely close connection between habit formation and embracing change and the 2 usually pass hand in hand. The essential goal of this ebook is training you the manner to form right conduct and that is less difficult while the way to embody trade. Change is clearly a massive part of carrying out success as it takes you via a sequence of tales all of which I find out pretty instructional. You get to open yourself up to a few form of attention which enhances your growth and progress.

EFFECTIVE STEPS TO TAKE IN LEARNING HOW TO EMBRACE CHANGE

An critical desire you could make for your lifestyles is that of reading a way to include alternate. I say this because I recognize that exchange is the best regular trouble in existence and with out it, nothing large will ever be finished. What you want to be aware is that you may in no way run away from alternate, and that the handiest way to make your life extra huge is thru acknowledging and embracing it. This part of the e book will take you through a journey of boom as it enlightens you on specific techniques to learn how to embody change. It pursuits at permitting people installed mind the reality that the surprising isn't always to be feared as it may be your handiest danger to make a distinction. Below are a number of the statistics to help you adapt to and embody exchange effects:

• Understanding that change is inevitable: This is surely especially real and as a whole lot as we also can insist on locking ourselves in our consolation zones, there comes a time when we're compelled to simply accept alternate. Our disability to in truth acquire that change is inevitable, is what makes plenty of us go through life having in no way lived to our complete ability. By accepting the inevitability of exchange we're definitely making organized ourselves to high-quality address it while it occurs. You received't fight it whilst it takes area however alternatively method it with enthusiasm.

• Initiate change: It can be simpler for all and sundry to cope with change if they may be folks that initiated it aligning it with all their dreams and desires. Change always seems like a nightmare while we are not a part of it, this manner you're permitting your life to improvement down a poor direction. Initiating trade includes working closer to what we aspire, if it's miles in your career lifestyles reputation on the sort of factors an awesome way to decorate that form of fulfillment. Don't simply sit down and look in advance to things to take place on their non-public, but as an alternative combat on your goals. The entire idea within the decrease again of beginning alternate is so you can create an attention and by manner of doing this you get to create greater possibilities.

• Exercise gratitude: With gratitude an person will constantly have the coronary

coronary coronary heart to consist of change. This is a danger that permits you to recognise all this is taking region for your lifestyles such that change to you may be considered as a growing opportunity. An assessment of things which might be fairly preferred to your lifestyles lets in you to be the form of person who yearns for development and through that, you discover ways to consist of exchange.

• Commit to personal boom: When you interest your all on non-public boom, there can be now not some element in you with a purpose to compromise that. You is probably greater than willing to surely take delivery of exchange due to the reality a massive part of you is aware about it's miles the first-rate way to open your self to opportunities developing your opportunities for non-public boom. The thing is, that even as you include exchange you begin mastering extra about who you're and the manner to great function. Such popularity permits for a much happier and similarly awesome lifestyles.

• View life thru specific eyes: This is a superb deal approximately seeing matters from a completely unique attitude. Avoid your antique and proscribing mind which misinform your way of handling trade. To gather this I should inspire you to workout extraordinary wondering as this offers one a more healthful method toward life.

Chapter 12: Identifying Bad Habits And Getting Rid Of Them

It will become a good deal much less difficult an high-quality way to put off horrific conduct as fast as you've got were given an know-how of what they may be. There are all varieties of behavior people hold and it can be at times very hard to apprehend those for you to gain you, and those that only break you. A terrible dependancy is described as a awful behavior sample that could have an effect in your journey to high-quality your desires and goals. Bad behavior are not properly however as an possibility quite poor to our highbrow and physical fitness.

It is continually tough to do away with horrible behavior because of the reality they always supply one instantaneous, faux satisfaction and a notable instance is procrastination. The second you push ahead a challenge you can enjoy correct about resting or exciting at that specific time but what you gained't realize is which you are honestly hurting your destiny. Another component is that the ones varieties of behavior take too much manipulate of someone's thoughts and lifestyles. You also can additionally have a propensity to just accept as real with that is how subjects are meant to be however the reality is that there is mostly a way out of that.

The forms of behavior are very one-of-a-kind from every unique and it received't be as difficult to differentiate the brilliant from the awful.

Below are examples of lousy conduct that need to be averted so as for one to beautify their large health and properly-being:

• Spending an excessive amount of time searching TV: This is one of the bad behavior that may be very tempting. As tons as one also can furthermore sense notable sitting at the couch for as prolonged because it takes to have a look at movies, it comes with its very very personal risks too. For one, there are immoderate possibilities of developing wonderful ailments having decreased your physical hobby. Our our our our bodies had been designed on this kind of manner that you need to exercise and pass spherical so that every one one-of-a-type body features are controlled and done efficiently. When you watch too much tv your productiveness is reduced and your thoughts moreover has a dishonest to be very inactive and slow.

• Overspending: A important supply of stress within the global these days is idea to be financial problems. When you're continually in the dependancy of spending an excessive amount of then it way you may emerge as in some of debt, or will lack sufficient coins to stay a comfortable existence. This you need to recognise can also need to bring about lots strain and fear which in the long run impacts an man or woman's extensive fitness and health. According to analyze, financial pressure has been showed to be a leading reason of insomnia, despair, ulcers, alcoholism and so forth.

•	Unhealthy consuming: Unhealthy consuming behavior continuously consist of severa bad results on each your mind and body. Eating correct meals is what contributes to a healthful way of life and is exactly what absolutely everyone need to do. It can be a laugh and all to devour an excessive amount of speedy food, but this can attain this plenty harm to your frame. It is probably a motive of extended frame weight, coronary coronary heart disease, diabetes and plenty of others.. Healthy food is also regarded to assemble one's thoughts and also you consequently need it for powerful widespread performance.

• Skipping breakfast: Breakfast is taken into consideration due to the reality the most critical meal of the day that have to be prioritized always. Skipping it'll have an effect for your weight, blood sugar, and power levels. Having slept for hours the frame will in fact need food early in the morning. This way you could hold on with all the day's sports feeling energized and in an super temper.

• Complaining: There is that this agency of folks that are constantly complaining about the whole lot in preference to showing gratitude to some component they've got going on of their existence. The truth is that you may't discover blessings whilst you are not able to recognize what you have got or in which you already are. With gratitude one opens themselves as lots as such plenty of opportunities and possibilities.

• Comparing yourself to others: This is every different terrible addiction that each one want to try to avoid as it damages our self perception and conceitedness. The component is, that there will commonly be a person who is better than you in a single certain area, and the extra you preserve evaluating yourself, the greater miserable you turn out to be. This is because of the truth you could in no way discover inner peace and could commonly want to be higher in the entirety.

• Living within the past: We all recognize that the top notch way to stay our lives is by means of the use of specializing within the present moment. The past is long long gone and the destiny might not come so why not interest your all in taking issue in the time you have got were given now. This dependancy wherein one constantly concentrates on beyond regrets can be quite adverse. You will continuously be sad and disturbed and this influences the way you do topics. It is wise of you if you are capable of forgive yourself and one of a kind human beings for ache precipitated in the past.

•   Never setting your self first: This is an act wherein one is continuously putting super human beings's wishes, feelings and goals earlier in their own. You might also grow to be being taken gain of because of the reality you appear to treasure others extra than you. It is considered a lousy dependancy because of the reality ends in low self-esteem, permits for self-forget about about approximately, and one compromises their non-public happiness. As a "human beings-pleaser" you may be living your lifestyles for others and this means loss of pleasure and success to your detail.

•   Drug addiction: This is one lousy dependancy that affects your relationships and moreover harms your very very own fitness. An alcoholic for example, also can spend lots time ingesting and any interaction with circle of relatives and friends won't be quality. Drug dependancy generally affects your way of dwelling and you can in no way perform efficaciously each in your private or expert existence. A big part of your life is usually messed up and you could turn out to be very depressed and dangerous.

•   Living one-of-a-kind human beings's goals: As an man or woman you want to continuously have your very very own definition of fulfillment. If you don't then it way you'll be living wonderful people's goals and definition of the word. This manner you may never advantage achievement and could clearly be residing in circles without getting anywhere profitable.

• Too a notable deal stressful: such pretty some humans are a sufferer of annoying all of the time even over little or no subjects. One issue about excessive disturbing is that it's going to have an effect on your highbrow, physical, and emotional fitness. You normally have a tendency to stay an sad life due to the truth your mind is concerned inside the awful constantly.

• Sleeping for few hours: Not getting enough sleep is probably the worst detail one does to themselves. It isn't first-rate approximately the amount but most significantly the fantastic of sleep. If you want to manual an lively and pleasurable life then go to bed early and awaken early. Sleep plays a big characteristic in our present day nicely being because it influences how we anticipate and also how our frame feels.

• Working too much: If you word which you are usually worn-out and depressed then it approach you are going for walks greater hard. No be counted how hard your work is there have to continuously be some time spent for rest because the frame absolutely goals that.

• Focusing at the negative issue of existence: there is lots greater to lifestyles than the lousy subjects which can be taking place. When you maintain focusing at the terrible then the entirety else feels terrible. It is terrific that one receives to count on and enjoy terrific approximately life for them stay a wholesome way of existence.

• Undermining yourself: anyone have strengths and weaknesses and setting yourself down because you've got failed in a few aspect is incorrect. People want to constantly stand tall and agree with in themselves no matter the shape of troubles they're going through.

HOW TO BREAK BAD HABITS

It is possible for actually all of us to prevent horrific behavior or even replace them with effective ones. That being said, it constantly takes time to do this; this can show to be overwhelming, but you want to understand that terrible conduct harm your reputation in addition to your career capability, and therefore it's nicely truely worth it to install your try to overcome them. Use the techniques mentioned underneath to break those negative behavior on your life.

Design a Plan

Research has display that when someone creates a aware plan, it assists the character to get began at the entire gadget of overcoming terrible conduct. You need to devise a concrete plan to make this a truth. A certain manner to go approximately that is with the useful resource of way of incorporating a dependancy-breaking approach into your personal dreams. This will assist you to continuously evaluation your improvement, and art work on the conduct which can be most poor to those which might be least detrimental. Once you've got advanced a plan, upload milestones and activates into your Action software program or To-Do List. This will act as a reminder of the matters that you want to obtain.

Develop Self-Awareness and Self-Control

Research has showed that normal self-vigilance is paramount to getting rid of any addiction. This is completed with the useful resource of reminding your self approximately the significance of breaking the lousy dependancy and searching your self for slip-ups. To absolutely accomplish this, you need to art work for your power of will and willpower; this will allow you to broaden the incentive in addition to the staying strength to save you the behavior.

You additionally want to assemble self-awareness a great way to hold your interest of your mind and the manner you feel. This is the simplest manner that you'll be able to understand your terrible behaviors in the first place.

Always Use the Right Approach

A extensive form of humans discover it hundreds more effective to prevent a addiction proper away, whilst others opt to restrict the conduct regularly over time. Therefore, it is important to apply a viable technique that works correctly on your state of affairs. The preference which you make will possibly rely on the form of conduct that you need to prevent.

Put Obstacles in Place

Psychologists say that people can prevent awful conduct through manner of putting limitations in areas that prevent them from indulging the addiction. You additionally have to persuade smooth of the places, people, or situations that would motive the terrible conduct.

Engage yourself in Positive Habits

In such an entire lot of occasions, you may prevent awful conduct through manner of manner of replacing them with nice ones. For instance, supposing you want to prevent being a critic, to eliminate this dependancy, you could decide to make a conscious try and ensure which you reward extraordinary people as an possibility.

Make Sure That You Reward Yourself

To save you a horrific conduct, it's miles effective to recompense yourself for engaging in the pleasant conduct. The purpose for doing that is due to the fact at the same time as you harm the vintage dependancy you may pass over the dopamine surge; now, the reward will compensate for that as a substitute. With time, the adjustment to your brain will begin to associate new, amazing behavior with the dopamine surge that come from the compensations. The worthwhile strategy and what you praise your self with is totally as an awful lot as you, absolutely make certain that the reward includes a few aspect that you truly enjoy. Once you have got got installed the best dependancy, there will be no want for the rewards to be made constantly.

Involve Others

In give up, it's far beneficial for people who want to interrupt lousy conduct to consider asking other people, colleagues, pals, or perhaps circle of relatives individuals, to help you save you the poor behavior. You need an brilliant way to percentage your goals with them, and inquire approximately the right strategies of coping with relapse. This will continuously make the method to be greater responsible, and it will additionally enhance your motivation.

Chapter 13: Goal Setting

It is through intention putting that one is capable of put in location and discover ways to exercise ideal conduct. It's however, generally tough for humans to recognize a way to set dreams efficaciously just so they may be capable of observe via them. A purpose as you can already recognize is an objective one wants to meet and aim setting is even as you deliver all your goals a sure time frame and have in mind the specific strategies of reaching them. Having desires may be very useful whilst you need to put off horrible behavior and domesticate nicely ones.

There is so much power in purpose placing, it being a device of thinking about your shape of destiny and motivating your self to reveal all of your visions into reality. The whole intention placing technique gives one an possibility to pick wherein they need to be in life and the manner they want to live it. As you location desires you're able to understand the type of behavior you consider are aligned to the success of unique goals.

If you have got got had been given been strolling tough however don't seem to get anywhere profitable then it can be that your route has not been well described. This approach you haven't taken some time to understand who you want to be and aren't aware of how you can lead your lifestyles as a manner of achieving your desires. It will become much less complicated for you in case you take some time and set dreams allowing them to be your source of motivation and path. If it's far about changing your behavior then write that down and provide yourself a time body for the success.

Successful people in each subject understand how essential it's far to always set dreams and this consists of athletes, entrepreneurs, etc. They understand that dreams form them into the individual they want to be and is what they skip returned to once they enjoy topics are not heading inside the right path. Life can be very hard when you lack direction and additionally whilst you lack cause. With dreams in thoughts you may constantly wake up knowledge you want to paintings inside the direction of sure achievements and this may be a super destruction and you gained't have time to adopt horrible behavior.

The motive why many are for the concept of placing desires in existence is because it offers a person prolonged-term imaginative and prescient and quick-time period motivation. An important hassle is that it enables you focus your understanding and equally distribute your assets as a way of making the most from your life.

There is a hyperlink amongst aim setting and addiction formation due to the fact via aim placing one creates an attention of negative conduct and focuses their hobby on building amazing conduct. It is all approximately converting each aspect of your existence such that each one regions are sincerely endorsed. In putting desires make sure that they will be sharp, in reality defined and measurable. The method of purpose placing entails having a big photo of all your desires, damage them into smaller goals and then positioned down plans on a manner to gather them.

To accumulate success anybody need to take goal placing very substantially due to the fact thru them one turns into particularly targeted and also you will be inclined to be more on pinnacle of factors of your entire life. It will advocate trade to you acquired't be tough to deal with as you can have already initiated and anticipated it. Goals are precisely what absolutely everyone need in identifying whether or not we are making development in life or now not.

EFFECTIVE GOAL SETTING AND ACHIEVEMENT TIPS

Setting dreams is not a hard problem, however to ensure that you do it successfully you then definately definately want to understand some of the guidelines that permits you to behave as your guideline. These will help you recognise what is required of you and what it manner to set the excellent desires. Setting dreams is one trouble and accomplishing them is each different, one ought to therefore be geared up with the proper tools to do every. Explained under are guidelines to help you to effects and efficaciously set and obtain all your desires:

• When putting desires you want to have every brief-term and prolonged-time period because of the reality existence is often a step at a time and need to allow the smaller dreams to guide into the larger ones.

• Another important element is which you need to have sensible and measurable dreams. This approach having in thoughts the desires which might be surely ability and which you have the property and the capability required.

• Express all of your desires positively just so each part of you can feel first-rate approximately achieving them.

• It is critical that one devices desires for you to inspire them as that is all about ensuring that your dreams are very important to you, and could upload loads price to your lifestyles as quickly as they may be done.

• It is essential which you have all of your dreams in writing, as this makes them tangible, or clearly actual. You received't overlook about them and could have a reference component while tracking progress.

• All the set dreams should be time sure as this locations some proper stress on you and consequently you obtained't look in advance to topics to appear on their very own however will as an alternative positioned ahead all attempt to ensure that you are in fact pushing closer to know-how all your dreams and dreams.

• Before you vicinity desires, you want to investigate your internal-self as a manner of figuring out what you need precisely, and then being privy to the specific subjects with the intention to convey happiness into your existence.

• You need to make certain which you stay with your desires but also be open to adjustments with the useful resource of technique of making an allowance for flexibility. As life movements such a lot of subjects change and this could name an amazing way to make a few adjustments on some unique desires.

• One desires to often asses their desires so as for them to apprehend whether or not or no longer they will be putting in enough try to reap them and the way a ways they've got lengthy beyond. Through this you can moreover know whether or not or not the ones dreams are though what you need to gain.

• As you vicinity dreams, it in fact lets in to make certain which you have motion plans in area actually so the entire process of attaining them can be that a bargain less complex.

•   Believe to your desires and on your potential to gain them, so that you can create amazing thoughts and attitude making it less complex on the way to attain your desires.

Chapter 14: Self Discipline

Personal improvement is largely determined by the use of one's improvement in strength of will. Absence of this easy problem can bring about the degeneration of 1's improvement. In order to end up the person who you want to be on this life, or advantage some thing it is that you need, you have to be self-disciplined. Self-area exists in severa office work, this includes; staying electricity, perseverance, self-control, wondering in advance than acting, completing any undertaking that you begin to art work on, and moreover the potential to carry out one's selections and plans, irrespective of barriers, hardships, or inconvenience.

Self-location moreover manner the functionality to look at restraint; the functionality to live a long way from unhealthy more of some thing that might bring about negative consequences to your life. A key function of strength of thoughts, is the power to abstain from immediately or proper now satisfaction and gratification, on the manner to benefit some thing greater or greater exciting consequences, despite the fact that it can require greater strive in addition to greater time.

This normally used time period frequently motives some resistance and ache at the same time as noted; that is because of the inaccurate notion that it refers to three detail that is hard to accumulate, ugly, or something that has a number of task and regularly requires a number of sacrifice. But in reality, implementation and reputation of self area does not require strenuous efforts; it could result in exhilaration, plus, the advantages are astonishing.

Genuine strength of mind is neither a restrictive nor a punitive manner of lifestyles like a few humans take delivery of as actual with; it's miles have been given not whatever to do with being dogmatic or opinionated. It's just in truth the manifestation of internal strength and staying energy, this is vital for handling our day after day affairs and moreover for the attaining of desires. Self-trouble refers back to the authority to workout energy over one's self. It is the electricity to hold one's person underneath manipulate. The phrase in itself denotes self- over one's mind, inner desires, words, and moves. This is the type of manipulate that any decided character need to exercise over his lifestyles.

HOW TO BE SELF DISCIPLINED

By executing the strategies discussed beneath and through using way of using them unswervingly, you may be succesful to build up brilliant strength of will, superhuman energy of mind, and the functionality to accumulate some thing you place out to perform.

Meditation

Practicing conscientious meditation for severa minutes on a each day basis day can truely raise your strength of will to acquire electricity of will; the exercise of meditation builds up grey don't forget range mainly regions of the human thoughts in which feelings are regulated in addition to the device of choice making.

Exercise

Every day you studies greater approximately the blessings of exercise, the more you will undergo in thoughts it as obligatory. Not simplest does exercising increase one's highbrow standard usual overall performance, fitness, sleep great and temper, it additionally reduces frame fat ratio, tension levels, in addition to the possibilities of becoming ill. Even if it technique that you perform a little exercising for approximately 5 minutes every day, you may honestly take a look at some difference.

There's generally some factor which you love to do; for instance, if you find on foot on a treadmill insufferable, avoid doing it, discover a few thing that you love to do(as long as you genuinely sweat inside the approach), and make sure that you make that precise workout a ordinary detail of your lifestyles.

If you're the type of character who does not like workout, then maybe you haven't decided the right form of exercise that fits you. Never allow your inner self accept as true with that you have been now not made for exercise.

Accountability

Truth be advised, this term might not be the maximum engaging word within the

English vocabulary. However, the concept it represents is distinctly powerful. The belief it represents ensues that when we're left to our non-public plans, it's commonplace to provide you justification now not to perform a little component.

Take a second to be real with your self; most of the reasons we make are honestly pretexts that we make to stay contented and keep away from doing what we have to be doing. The method to this debacle is quite easy: expand strategies to your existence a good way to preserve you at better requirements; strategies as a way to inhibit you from formulating excuses.

There are some of strategies of reaching this. Discussed underneath are some few alternatives to consider:

• Get your self an responsibility-friend, a fitness center associate, art work next to a friend or a coworker, get a educate, create or join a mastermind organization, etc.

• No don't forget what system you appoint, the important thing rely right here is that the technique need to remove your potential to make excuses and procrastinate, and that it moreover makes you adhere on your plans and maximum values.

Remove Distractions and Temptations

Generally citing, human beings are exposed to temptation every day, it's part of our every day reviews. Especially in our global, we are surrounded every day, with the useful resource of extra immoderate temptations than ever earlier than in history.

To make topics worse, Search engines like Google or Bing and so on. Make it viable for us to get proper of get entry to to any information that we are searching for for within the international internal a rely of seconds. Entertainment web websites like NETFLIX and YouTube are full of exciting, interesting and funny movies. The social web sites that we sign up in arise so far every second; our clever phones are complete of apps as well as exciting matters.

Understanding this, it's essential which you make a decision out a manner to protect your self against an entire lot of those distractions. In order to try this you can need to;-

• Identify and study what your not unusual distractions are.

• Develop a plan to mitigate those distractions

Once you are able to influence clear of those temptations, you may effects direct all your power of will to reaching wonderful topics collectively with self-control, other than fighting the impulse to eliminate all yet again.

BENEFITS OF SELF-DISCIPLINE

Self-problem is handiest a non-public path towards lifestyles. Self-area isn't an version in life but rather a dependancy. Therefore you could certainly exercising self-control with a purpose to obtain a better lifestyles. So many a achievement humans nowadays characteristic their achievement to electricity of mind. Self-location in existence encompasses severa virtues like staying wholesome, being focused, and furthermore guidance clean of problems. These days, strength of will techniques seem like one of the maximum critical lifestyles competencies. As a count of reality, strength of mind is a major difficulty by way of manner of using which people use to choose others. Therefore it is suitable to embody self-discipline in your life. The advantages of strength of will in existence consists of but isn't limited to:-

• Developing recognition

• Gaining recognize from others

• Better fitness

• Better Education

• Staying active

• Being glad & getting topics completed

• Having greater unfastened time within the day

• Tension & strain unfastened

Self-vicinity also assists you to:-

• Execute ensures which you made.

• Prevent yourself from acting rapidly.

• Carry on with a task, even after the preliminary rush of exhilaration has dwindled away.

- Overcome procrastination and idleness.

- Carry on together collectively along with your food plan, and overcoming the temptation of ingesting risky elements.

- Exercise, swim, or walk, each time your thoughts deceives you to live at your own home and watch films.

- Beat the dependancy of being preoccupied with an excessive amount of TV.

- Wake up early.

- Meditate on a ordinary basis.

Chapter 15: Developing Good Habits

In your try to reap the fantastic form of lifestyles via all of your reminiscences and conditions it actually allows to maintain authentic behavior. These are what is going to shape and assist you interest your all into know-how that. This a long way you comprehend there are true behavior and horrible behavior and it's miles your responsibility to make certain that you put off the awful ones and domesticate suitable ones. It is handiest via trouble that an man or woman can flow from point A to B and you're first-class disciplined when you have particular conduct. It isn't always difficult to build and preserve actual conduct and with the aid of manner of following the stairs under you'll be able to gather that:

Analyze Your Current Habits

This is an crucial step to take as it permits making a decision the form of conduct you've got. One gets to type through the said terrible conduct that have been the cause for their loss of improvement, and the exceptional ones that need to be superior upon. At this element, you will have an concept of in which to begin from in growing perfect conduct as a manner of improving your chosen well-being.

Identify the Kind of Habit You Want To Develop

Having recounted the difference amongst appropriate and horrific behavior, the subsequent step for you is being aware about the proper dependancy you are trying to introduce in your life. Have an inner knowledge of why it's miles important and the kind of distinction it will make on your lifestyles. This is quality accomplished even as you understand the regions of your life that want development as it is through this that you establish the form of behavior which can be appropriate.

Commitment

It is critical that on every occasion you want to advantage some trouble you deliver it your all, and this is approximately committing to that trade. Ensure that every part of you is willing to artwork in the direction of developing the extremely-present day dependancy and which you are equipped to stay with it. This will encompass having the right mind, emotions, and attitude within the path of it.

Identify Obstacles

In any undertaking one partakes there'll virtually be tremendous stressful situations and limitations that are probably to be encountered. In the device of dependancy formation, it's far very vital which you create an cognizance of the possible disturbing situations and prepare your self inside the incredible way possible to overcome them. A ideal example is on the identical time as you want to start a healthy exercising everyday, part of you may need to give up before you get far and you want to have out of doors sources of motivation to hold you heading in the right route.

Use Visualization

This is an critical device in relation to dependancy formation, what it does is that it acts as an internal deliver of motivation. Picture yourself in a scenario in which you are already exercising the addiction and the way simply your life has been endorsed. You can also moreover try using affirmations which can be noted to carry related photographs into thoughts which in turn act on motivating, energizing, and scary. The moment this dependancy will become a part of your highbrow and emotional being it's miles going to be less hard so you can workout it.

Regularly Practice The Habit

It is probably very crucial which you workout the dependancy extra often and it's going to with time turn out to be part of you. If you need to usually meditate then do it till it comes absolutely and it's going to never sense as a project. The more one does some detail then your body gets used to it and you may continuously be looking beforehand to it. This is due to the fact you begin seeing the advantages of retaining the chosen addiction and the way certainly your existence is transforming nad you will consequently no longer want to stop.

Find Support

In constructing new conduct it's far continuously essential for one to have outside useful resource and this will be family or buddies. Make them aware of your goal and how crucial it will probably be to you. Ask them to constantly be on the advent out in making sure that you are certainly exercising the high-quality conduct. These are critical human beings on your existence who I endure in thoughts can be greater than willing to cheer you on and moreover will will let you realise whilst matters aren't going as required.

Reward Yourself

You also can in reality assist your self to have applicable conduct with the useful resource of locating healthful techniques to praise your self. This ought to constantly be completed any time you recognise you are making development in preventing terrible conduct and building new ones. The rewards should be topics that make you experience truely correct as through this you may always paintings closer to accomplishing the rewards.

Examples of correct conduct:

Highlighted below are some examples of suitable behavior that I be given as proper with even as exercised will enhance all areas of someone's life. They purpose super components and I recognize they are all worth some time.

- Regular exercise

- Positive wondering

- Goal placing

- Practice frame and mind relaxation

- Living within the gift second

- Have amusing and don't artwork all the time

- Take the steps and not the elevator

- Have small talks

- Drink 8 ounce glass of water every morning the immediate you awaken

- Always pass for wholesome meals selections

- Wake up early each day

- Listen to and have a look at motivational materials

- Use affirmations

- Love your self

- Exercise gratitude

- Take dangers

- Save enough cash thru maintaining off overspending

Chapter 16: Advantages Of Good Habits

It can enjoy brilliant and first-rate whilst you exercise some new precise conduct that assist you to gain a massive cause. When you furthermore may additionally examine new conduct you are changing your existence for the better. The powerful changes you consist of to your each day lifestyles will decide the way you're going to develop and enhance in each your expert and personal existence. There are a number of excellent conduct you could encompass for your life and a number of them encompass cleansing and organizing your own home, workout often, meditating, eating greater stop end result and veggies, and so on. These authentic conduct can exchange your life and a few gadget together with electricity of will, electricity of will and many others may be used whilst seeking to encompass any new addiction in your every day recurring.

Healthy behavior don't simply come into your life and proper away in form on your time table, consequently, you want to apprehend the proper skills you need that the brand new addiction calls for. If you actually need to be greater wholesome, greater active, active, green, centered, prepared and additional a success, then it's miles vital to consist of particular conduct on your life. There are many advantages of real conduct and some of them are defined below:

You Are In Charge Of Your General Health

Changing your way of life with the aid of the use of way of such as powerful behavior such as workout, consuming healthful elements, and meditating will help in improving your bodily and intellectual fitness. The most difficult behavior to perform are the ones ones related to fitness and fitness. When you have got got already mastered a manner to shape and use new conduct to exchange your existence, you'll be in entire control of your intellectual similarly to bodily health. For example, you could start changing your weight loss plan or take the stairs in desire to the improve. Try converting your terrible behavior even if you don't sense like doing it.

When you experience confused, depressed, overwhelmed, or irritating; you need to try to encompass competencies which can assist alternate your highbrow behavior on the manner to totally decorate your view on existence. Some remarkable conduct that would assist decorate your highbrow health include visualization, respiratory frivolously, affirmations, meditation, yoga, quality wondering, and lots greater. For the ones conduct to effectively enhance your highbrow, physical, and emotional fitness then they need to be instilled in your everyday life.

You Will Be Creative and More Productive

When you've got got had been given determined to consist of a sure immoderate nice addiction for your each day existence, you'll start being organized and grow to be greater powerful. Some correct behavior that might assist you be more effective embody waking up early, writing brief-term and lengthy-time period desires, sorting your emails, organizing your place of job, analyzing motivational books and magazines, and so on. These conduct are essential as you will continuously recognize in which you want to be, what you need to do, and wherein some of your important subjects are placed. Time wastage may be decreased and you'll have greater time to do various things which might be more essential. Good behavior make us to be more prepared, more powerful, more creative, smarter, and open to many opportunities that would assist us gain success.

Strengthens Your Relationship

You can create a dependancy of putting out collectively together with your family on weekends, spending great time together with your companion and discussing circle of relatives troubles, and hugging your accomplice every morning in advance than you go to art work. Communication is critical to a protracted-lasting dating and that's why it's important a superb manner to sit down down collectively together along with your companion and decide what obligations you have to do collectively or offer you with an idea of wherein you'll be going for a holiday. By sharing the entirety and discussing each single trouble affecting your dating, you will assemble accept as true with, care, and love inside the courting. When it includes finance it's crucial to talk about at the side of your accomplice on how you must spend the cash and finances collectively. These appropriate conduct will bring the two of you further for your children closer together.

Improves Your Leaning

If you need to do some component exceptional to your lifestyles then, you need to have exceptional skills that permit you to make suitable behavior be a part of your existence. It could possibly gain a detail in which you may want extra competencies at the manner to perform your work efficaciously, this may pressure you to take a certain path and beautify your abilties. Adapting new studying talents will will can help you be in a higher characteristic to perform any art work hobby. There also are other things you can want to study e.G. Mastering - a present day game, a manner to play guitar, the manner to write down a ebook, or even learning a modern-day language. It is feasible to conform the ones and exceptional wonderful behavior as long as the dependancy ability you need to investigate and live dedicated to it.

Improves Your Finances

If you are overspending, in debt, need to shop for a new car, need to preserve for university, or need to transport on a vacation; then you definately need to comply new conduct that will let you attain these things. The behavior which could help enhance your price range include managing your cash, spending tons much less, and saving. Set a brand new dependancy of saving a given quantity every day, week, or month and in the long run you may do some detail you don't forget to do with the cash.

Chapter 17: Good Habits For Success

Many humans go through their lives, envying special people's achievement; now not comprehending all the difficult art work as well as screw ups that they encounter. Successful human beings constantly appear to have their 'act' together; they always appear like composed, whilst others are just suffering to get through the day.

Question is, is this because of mere unique fortune? Are they extra clever? Were they raised in aristocracy? Well, the answer is "NOT EVERY LAST ONE OF THEM." Success isn't always confined on your IQ degree, race, or maybe the scale of your wallet. And till now, there's no denying that there are sure traits that a success human beings have, which helped them to get wherein they'll be in the interim. Discussed below are a number of the ones traits;

Read a Lot

Through reading, one is in a role to analyze from the shortcomings as well as the successes of others. When you desire to do some component with your existence, in preference to taking movements hastily even as relying on your guts and intuition as your compass, studying will offer you with a highbrow map to bypass all the minor errors one of a kind humans make in life. They kind out the training they analyze and preserve the information for future software program

Wake up early

This precise dependancy isn't easy to domesticate; a superb idea can be to test with numerous strategies which includes alarm clocks, or final your lighting one hour earlier than you fall asleep, and so forth.

Exercise

Even although a hit human beings have all the belongings that they'll ever require to maintain fitness and live wholesome, they though exercising on a every day foundation; exercise is a part of their each day regular. Apart from fitness and health, exercise improves your reminiscence, minimizes pressure, and moreover ensures that your thoughts stays healthy. Research has hooked up that exercising can sincerely decorate productivity in addition to creativity. And don't forget that it additionally raises your IQ.

Persevere

This is the only problem that distinguishes specialists from wannabes. It is through perseverance that an character is capable of open themselves as an awful lot as greater possibilities in lifestyles. There will generally be demanding conditions and obstacles, however with a coronary coronary coronary heart this is inclined to fight, you are confident of reaching greater heights. You need no longer compromise all your goals and dreams in reality due to the fact you may't persevere or are not able to take dangers.

Meditate

Research findings advise that meditation alleviates ache, anxiety, and additionally prevents despair. Mediation has the ability to decorate your capability to awareness. For the beginner inside the worldwide of meditation, you may increase the dependancy thru manner of concentrating in your breath for approximately five mins; that is the same old vicinity to begin of newbie 'meditators'.

Minimize distractions

It is essential which you normally attempt tough to be in environments or round individuals who permit for your boom and development. Choose inspiring environments and sports activities activities in case you need to always stay on course.

Donate

Most a success human beings take their time to provide once more to their network via donations, charities, and volunteering.

Work tough

Successful human beings are devoted to the matters that they do. In lifestyles you may unearth shortcuts, but you could in no way avoid the tough art work required to make bigger the foundation of your goals.

Don't spoil your conduct!

This continuously motivates a success people to maintain happening and it's miles all about sticking to the great conduct regardless of how tough instances are. If you're aware about the conduct that push you ahead then maintain them the least bit expenses.

GOOD HABITS FOR HEALTH

Although there may be no guarantee for a superbly healthful and glad existence, if you make a decision to paste to the ones ten steps, there can be a danger if you want to enhance your fitness and popular tremendous of life. If but making a decision to push aside them, there may be a opportunity that you'll be taking a large gamble collectively in conjunction with your bodily, emotional further to intellectual nicely being.

Include Omega-3 Fatty Acids wealthy meals for your Diet

Apart from the reality that the ones oils and acids are splendid assets of protein and food that has low ranges of saturated fat, moreover they reduce the chance of coronary coronary heart illness. Popular alternatives encompass lake trout, mackerel, herring, albacore tuna, sardines and salmon. Other options embody tofu, canola, soybeans, flaxseed and walnuts. There are some evidences that show those fatty acids usually soothe overactive immune systems, lessen allergies, eczema, asthma, and severa autoimmune troubles.

Take Breakfast Every Morning

Study consequences show that folks that devour morning food commonly usually tend to get greater minerals and vitamins, and less portions of ldl ldl ldl cholesterol in addition to fat. This often results in a leaner, in shape body, that has low cholesterol levels and there's also lesser risk that you may overeat.

Get Enough Sleep

Sleep is vital for attaining super fitness in addition to emotional plus intellectual properly-being. Sleep deprivation can have an effect on your gaining knowledge of, memory and logical reasoning negatively.

Take Up A Hobby

Pick up hobbies and other relaxing sports which are typically a laugh. Such sports may additionally include; chicken searching, craftwork, sports activities activities, gambling cards, taking walks in parks, or maybe going to flea markets. The entertainment will assist you to stay a extra wholesome lifestyles and you'll be capable of easily recover from infection.

Practice Dental Hygiene

Did you understand that dental flossing can upload more than six years in your existence; of course if it's far finished collectively with sports activities and additionally if you surrender smoking. Scientists' suspect that the micro organism that normally motives dental plaque enters into the bloodstream and in some way reasons the contamination which blocks blood vessels and sooner or later brings about coronary heart disorder. Other studies have observed comparable links among this bacteria and starting issues, stroke, and diabetes.

Protect Your Skin

Scientists cite that the extraordinary way to look younger and additionally protect your pores and skin is with the useful resource of staying out of the solar. This is because of the reality the solar has ultraviolet rays which may be unstable; to the amount that would motive dryness, wrinkles, or maybe age spots. When your pores and skin receives overexposed to the ones rays, you may get sunburn, dilated blood vessels, pores and pores and skin texture changes, or even pores and skin cancers.

Drink Water and Eat Daily

Apart from being wholesome fluids, water and milk can also will let you shed some weight.

The water allows your joints to stay in movement; it is also useful for the right functioning of the vital frame organs consisting of the liver, kidney, mind and the coronary coronary heart.

The dairy merchandise have calcium that is important for robust tooth in addition to bones. Calcium can assist in stopping excessive blood stress, colon most cancers, kidney stones, and coronary coronary coronary heart illness.

Snack The Healthy Way

For a healthful diet it's far smart to have greater than five servings of fruits and vegetables on a daily basis. This will enhance your fitness, lessen the chance of a few cancers, decorate memory, beat signs and symptoms of getting old, decorate your immune device, and additionally sell coronary heart fitness.

Drink Tea

Tea has been set up to enhance one's reminiscence, in addition to prevent tooth cavities, coronary heart disorder and cancer.

Take A Daily Walk

An test which become completed on thirteen,00 people for 8 years indicated that people who walked for at least 1/2 an hour on a each day basis had a considerably decrease threat of premature lack of lifestyles as compared to people who not often did any shape of exercising.

GOOD HABITS FOR HAPPINESS

In order to domesticate happiness into your existence, you want to research and take a look at those set of behavior.

Forgive and Forget

This is critical for your very personal happiness; it frees you from negativity and gives your moral sense extra location for extremely good feelings to are dwelling.

Develop Kindness

This dependancy isn't always most effective contagious, however it will additionally make you a exceptional deal happier in case you attempted it. You'll be able to create sturdy bonds with those round you, nurturing positivity all round.

Be Grateful For What You Have

This will assist you to address pressure, growth exquisite feelings, and additionally will let you acquire your desires.

Dream Big

Never limit your capabilities, you need to be more exceptional and positive; thru those you could harness the electricity to achieve your choice.

Let pass of the Small Stuff

Happy individuals understand the significance of letting little irritations slide off their backs.

Don't Compare Yourself to Others

You are unique, and so is your life, consequently there is no want with a view to degree your personal existence with that of other people. Even if you decide to deal with your lifestyles to be higher than others, the choice will ultimately show to be damaging on your non-public happiness. Never nurture judgmental emotions or maybe terrible perspectives of superiority.

Chapter 18: Habit One 0 One

Do what a dependancy is?

You can also additionally have a indistinct concept; you may in reality expect it's a few aspect you over and over do, and that's real in pretty a few strategies, however the generation in the back of it is going a hint deeper than that, as with most topics in lifestyles.

So, what's a dependancy?

What is a Habit?

The definition of a dependancy is that this:

A regular tendency, one that is tough to give up, and one that is regularly sub-aware

A addiction is therefore a few element we do without even figuring out it, a few component we occasionally feel we want, and some problem which may be very tough to stop doing. Many people talk with smoking as a addiction, because it essentially fulfills that definition – it is difficult to not do once you begin, we regularly do it without virtually thinking about it, and it is something you revel in you need.

On the possibility hand, a dependancy can be a few element simple, some thing, like having a espresso first thing inside the morning, as it will become 2d nature, sub-aware, and consequently you don't experience super besides you indulge in your morning caffeine hit.

Think about the property you do on a regular foundation, the stuff you do each unmarried day without in reality thinking about it. We're no longer speaking about brushing your teeth and getting dressed, due to the reality this is habitual, and this is something definitely excellent; we're speaking about the subjects that you do without in reality wondering – do you continuously do a particular task a hard and fast way, due to the fact it's miles the excellent manner you feel you have completed it? This is a dependancy.

Of direction there are incredible strategies to do that task, methods which can be greater effective however you have got were given superior a addiction to do it that precise manner, and your thoughts will not will let you do it some other manner.

Habits are personal, it is why it's miles hard to offer you a specific listing of actual behavior and horrible conduct, or basically any addiction somewhere in the center! To provide you with an concept of in which we're going with this however, here are some examples:

•Smoking

•Fidgeting

•Touching things two times in advance than you may enjoy glad about leaving the room (every so often a signal of OCD, which we will talk about a touch more shortly)

•Washing fingers very well or greater than as soon as

•Nail biting

•Picking at nail polish

•Sarcasm (on occasion you certainly can't assist yourself!)

•Eating at certain instances of the day

•Eating a certain meals at a fantastic time of the day

•Sleeping at a splendid time of the day

•Exercising

As you can see, there may be now not some element in particular difficult approximately identifying a habit, due to the truth they're pretty smooth to look — some factor you do often, the same way, or occasionally on the identical time each day.

Are we born with behavior, or are we able to pick them up? You is probably asking your self that query, and the bottom line is that we are in fact now not born with conduct, they may be picked up and evolved through the years, occasionally via copying what others do (while we are children), or surely with the beneficial aid of being stimulated through the matters occurring in our lives, e.G. Dealing with pressure and smoking/drinking too much. This need to provide you a few desire that any bad behavior can be eliminated sincerely as resultseasily as you picked them up, with a bit work, of route.

As a brief piece of homework, maintain in mind what your conduct are, and write them down. Identifying them now, at this early stage, will assist you in your journey in the direction of figuring out which habits are terrible, and which can be unique, after which we are capable of offer you with the equipment to make adjustments where you need them. This workout isn't always alleged to be exhaustive, but simply run through your day in your mind, or perhaps your week in case you do splendid subjects on certain days, and write down your listing.

What is The Difference Between Routine and Habit?

We need to understand that there may be a completely actual distinction among your habitual, and your conduct. You shouldn't really need to alternate your ordinary if it is working for you, but there might be subjects you can put into effect into it, to kind out your conduct too – e.G.

Becoming some workout into your day, or making sure you get sufficient sleep.

Okay, permit's summarize, to make it all a chunk clearer.

Habit – Something you do often and time and again, within the same manner. It is a unconscious thing that you often don't recognize you're doing.

Routine – Your regular manner of going approximately your day, e.G. The movements you study in a fixed order, allowing you to get a interest completed, or to make it through your day successfully.

As you could see, the 2 are pretty similar in description, however there are vital versions. You can not without a doubt alternate your habitual too much without significantly affecting your day, however you can trade your conduct and beautify your day in many techniques.

A routine is critical, not best for children however additionally for adults. If you've got were given a routine you don't need to sit down down and make choices within the morning, delaying your day and causing strain. Routine moreover permits people feel calmer and further solid, this is why recurring is considered to be so essential for children specially.

The Close Relationship Between Habits and OCD (Obsessive Compulsive Disorder)

It's important to comment on this precise issue briefly, due to the fact conduct are occasionally a very actual symptom of OCD.

OCD stands for obsessive compulsive sickness, and this is a few thing it's miles becoming increasingly commonplace in our each day lives, as we set approximately searching for to deal with the stresses and lines that the cutting-edge day brings.

OCD is a intellectual fitness scenario, and it may have an effect on simply honestly every body. You will discover that a person who has OCD, or who is displaying signs of OCD will regularly have set behavior, and they revel in they need to do them, otherwise they cannot relaxation, and it sends them proper right into a panic, or a circle of hysteria.

OCD is really more approximately obsession and compulsion, due to the reality the mind tells the frame that they want to carry out a touch detail, e.G. Washing arms to the factor of excessive, or having to touch the door times in advance than taking walks thru it.

Whilst OCD is frequently made mild of, it is honestly a totally frightening and immoderate state of affairs, and if you enjoy you will be showing symptoms and signs and symptoms of this, you have to talk to your healthcare professional to are in search of for assist and recommendation.

As a preferred guiding precept, the number one signs of OCD are:

•Fear of germs or infection

•Fear of losing things or people

•Obsessive cleansing

•Constant anxiety

•Indulging inside the obsessive idea calms the character down, e.G. Cleansing arms makes the sensation of anxiety disappear for a quick time, earlier than it recurs

•Counting

•Repetition, e.G. Pronouncing the equal thing again and again

•Needing steady reassurance

•Checking topics excessively, e.G. Checking the door is locked, the gas is off

•Not being able to stand something that isn't perfectly located, e.G. A clock on the wall isn't quite straight

•Needing to have things in a hard and speedy order, e.G. The good deal orange in a single vicinity, the entirety inexperienced in a single area

These are the primary signs and symptoms of OCD, but it's vital to word that that may be a definitely private disorder, so in case you are in any respect involved, head to appearance your medical doctor for a communicate.

Of path, no longer sincerely everyone with a fixed quantity of behavior has OCD, due to the reality having behavior is everyday, it doesn't advocate you've got got OCD;

it's far whilst your behavior grow to be obsessive which you want to are searching out help.

Okay, now we understand what a addiction is, we've given some examples, and we've given you a short heads up and warning approximately the seriousness of OCD, permit's go directly to have a look at behavior in a chunk extra detail.

Chapter 19: Identifying Good Habits And Bad Habits

Everyone's concept of ideal and terrible is commonly pretty awesome, however at the entire, there are nice suggestions over what is taken into consideration bad and what's considered proper.

For example we recognize that supporting others is a brilliant element, and stealing is a terrible element – that is about morals, but identifying an awesome addiction and a awful one may be a bit extra tough in some times.

In our first financial disaster we suggested you to sit down down and write your very very own listing of conduct, and it would have amazed you a piece whilst you observed out what your personal conduct are! Don't be too freaked out approximately this however, it's pretty normal to now not clearly recognise the behavior you have got until you definitely sit down down and supply it some smooth concept.

We at the moment are going to head over a few examples of terrible conduct and proper conduct. Your next piece of labor is to take that listing of conduct you identified and region each one within the beauty of tremendous or lousy. Some is probably in a chunk of a grey region, neither precise nor awful, but it's critical to make a completely final desire, due to the truth from there you can preserve to expand it, or dispose of it.

Examples of Good Habits

•Cleaning up after you have got finished some thing, e.G. Not liking the idea of mess

•Washing your hands after going to the relaxation room

•Brushing your teeth within the morning and at night time (this is veering slightly into everyday territory, but as a dependancy, it's far a high-quality one to have in your health)

•Speaking great affirmations to start your day, beginning on a excellent word

•Doing a splendid deed every day, either for your self or a person else

•Removing your make up every night time

•Exercising frequently

•Eating fruit and vegetable each day

•Reading books

•Constantly seeking out to research a few factor new

•Respecting humans

•Smiling

•Going to mattress early

•Waking up early

•Being prepared, writing lists and getting your day by day obligations finished

•Drinking your quota of water steady with day

Examples of Bad Habits

•Smoking

•Drinking too often or too much (e.G. Binge consuming)

•Not thinking about the emotions of others

•Being lazy, e.G. Sleeping too much, no longer workout

•Being sarcastic

•Being unorganized

•Not paying bills on time

Chapter 20: How To Get Rid Of Bad Habits

Now we're going to get realistic!

Bad behavior are unhelpful, they motive dissatisfied and illness in lifestyles, and which could have an impact in your conventional fitness, properly being, and vanity.

So, how do you prevent a bad addiction, or maybe flip it right right into a tremendous?

It all is predicated upon on what the addiction is many times, and how terrible it is too.

Let's run through some eventualities.

Scenario 1

Bad addiction – Smoking

Why is it terrible? – Not actual for fitness, high-priced

Does it want to be changed or removed? — Eradicated

How can you change it? — Help from assist groups, scientific medical doctors, use of nicotine patches, gum, and sheer will strength

Scenario 2

Bad addiction — Seeking validation from others continuously

Why is it awful? — Because it erodes at your arrogance, chips at your ability to make selections independently, and ends in a negative thoughts-set

Does it need to be modified or eliminated? — Eradicated

How can you change it? — This is a scenario which goes to take time and effort, but you need to slowly start to reduce out the validation efforts, and consciousness at the wonderful in your lifestyles as a substitute. For example, in case you are soliciting for validation approximately the way you look constantly, ask your self why a person else's opinion subjects more than your personal. Focus at the positives, in preference to what you understand to be a terrible, and turn every horrible perception about your look right into a great one.

E.G. "My hair typically seems a big number" – that may be a horrific, but a first-class spin on this may be, "I even have lengthy, thick hair" – many human beings can also want to bounce thru hoops for extended, thick hair!

Changing terrible mindsets which require consistent validation proper into a first-class may be difficult and time consuming, however it's miles a journey that is greater than absolutely well worth it. Put truly, you don't need every body else's validation, exceptional your very very personal; it's flawlessly excellent to actually accept compliments and be glad approximately them, but never experience in conjunction with you want them to experience actual.

Scenario 3

Bad dependancy – Drinking alcohol often, or every so often excessively

Why is it terrible? – If you drink frequently, you are not always an alcoholic, however it isn't so brilliant in your health or mood each. Whilst a glass or wine or a lager is remarkable every now and then, eating each single day, or feeling which includes you want it to unwind or sense pinnacle, is a totally bad thing in reality.

Does it need to be changed or eliminated? – It is based upon at the severity of your addiction, but basic this can be modified, except there may be a critical dependancy

How can you exchange it? – Moderation is the essential factor proper proper here! Drink simplest at weekends, after which make certain you don't binge, due to the fact this is more poor to your fitness. Give yourself a deal with night time day out on a Friday or Saturday with pals and function some liquids then, but a few does not advise masses! It is higher to take pride in a tumbler of wine mid-week and a night time time out on the weekend, than it's far to move completely crazy on cocktails or vodka on a Saturday night time, feeling like you are loss of life a sluggish dying on Sunday, and then abstaining for the relaxation of the week. Moderation is essential right here.

Scenario four

Bad dependancy – Sleeping an excessive amount of or too little

Why is it horrific? – Too little sleep and you're sleep disadvantaged, too much sleep and also you enjoy gradual. You should possibly revel in like you may't win! Disrupted sleep styles aren't pinnacle in your mood or your frame, and at the same time as your frame is all around the vicinity with its resting patterns, it may't characteristic effectively. Your metabolism is likewise significantly tormented by how a whole lot relaxation you're, or aren't, getting.

Does this want to be changed or eliminated? – Modified

How can you exchange it? – Give your self a habitual and preserve on with it. For instance, make certain you're in bed at 11pm every night time at the same time as you need to paintings the subsequent morning, so that you sense clean when your alarm goes off, in desire to 1/2 asleep although. At weekends, superb, have a chunk of a lie in, however don't bypass over the pinnacle because of the truth this may moreover play havoc together with your body clock – treating your self to an extra hour is great.

If you are having too much sleep, i.E. You aren't going to bed until 5am and waking up at 3pm, it's time to offer your self a proper ordinary! This isn't always a healthy sample to have, except you're operating night time time shifts in which you definitely can't help it.

The bottom line is that you want to get the proper amount of sleep for you, and that could be a personal deal. Generally speaking, eight hours is the guideline of thumb of thumb of thumb.

These four eventualities are designed to reveal you that no longer all behavior want to be kicked out virtually, and that they'll be changed or modified barely.

Excess is one of the worst behavior you could have, because it wreaks havoc collectively along with your body and your life, at the same time as moderation brings calm and concord in your life and fitness traditional.

Turning a Negative Into a Positive

You could have heard this a thousand times earlier than – negativity breeds bad occasions, and positivity attracts great activities. You ought to name is the Law of Attraction, or you could honestly name it making your personal achievement, however the bottom line is that negativity isn't always any pinnacle for anybody.

A terrible attitude will absolute confidence have more in the manner of horrible conduct, so that you want to check out your precise method to life.

Are you a tumbler 1/2 of of whole or 1/2 empty form of person?

If you're half empty, it's time to start operating toward positivity, and probable use affirmations and high excellent wondering that will help you for your endeavors.

For every horrible idea you've got got, do that:

•Identify that the belief you're having is horrific

•Identify whether or not or now not the idea is as fact, or an opinion/imaginative and prescient out of your very personal mind

•Turn it on its head, and create a best. For instance, in preference to questioning "it's raining again", expect "it's terrific to look rain occasionally". You can do that for every unmarried belief you've got, you simply want to get a bit progressive in your wondering!

• Repeat it till it seeps into your brain

• Repeat this approach for each single bad notion you've got

For some time that is going to revel in alien, because of the truth your mind isn't compelled to be immoderate first-class, it's miles used to considering the terrible first. You can also revel in a chunk exhausted on the start too, because questioning a hint more than you're used to, being aware of your thoughts, is tiring! The suitable information however is that once some time this may turn out to be 2nd nature, as you train your mind to suppose in a amazing way.

So, we've handled horrible behavior, allow's test your right conduct, hoping to stop our chat on a top notch be aware.

Chapter 21: How To Develop Good Habits

Having have been given this a protracted manner via our e-book, you could now be stimulated to % your life with fine behavior, kicking out or editing the bad habits in your life.

We have talked about lousy conduct in-depth, presenting you with situations on how you can exchange or alter them. The list you made in our first financial disaster should now be looking masses extra excessive first-class than it did on the start too, however you may probable need to feature some more positives on your listing.

How are you able to try this?

It's now not easy, it takes time, but it may genuinely be carried out!

Here's the way to boom a first-rate dependancy.

•What addiction do you need to increase? Do you want to workout extra frequently? Do you need to be extra privy to your actions concerning others? Do you need to discover ways to save coins in area of spend it?

•What is your motivation?Why do you want to enlarge this powerful addiction? You need to actually need it and be given as actual with it for yourself, in choice to it being some thing someone has suggested you which you want to do. Once you're truly inspired, the rest becomes a hint easier.

www.ingramcontent.com/pod-product-compliance
Lightning Source LLC
Chambersburg PA
CBHW062139020426
42335CB00013B/1257